Obedience &
B E Y O N D

Andrew Picklyk

 FriesenPress

Suite 300 - 990 Fort St
Victoria, BC, V8V 3K2
Canada

www.friesenpress.com

ISBN
978-1-4602-8932-7 (Hardcover)
978-1-4602-8933-4 (Paperback)
978-1-4602-8934-1 (eBook)

1. RELIGION

Distributed to the trade by The Ingram Book Company

Table of Contents

v   Introduction

1   Chapter One: What time is it?

11   Chapter Two: Beyond Obedience

17   Chapter Three: Beyond Request

23   Chapter Four: Beyond Telling

27   Chapter Five: Beyond Basic Labour

31   Chapter Six: Beyond One Talent

45   Chapter Seven: Beyond Healing

51   Chapter Eight: Beyond the First Level

63   Chapter Nine: Beyond Winning

73   Chapter Ten: Beyond Just Enough

79   Chapter Eleven: Beyond the Common (part one)

97   Chapter Twelve: Beyond the Common (part two)

113   Chapter Thirteen: Beyond Hospitality

125   Chapter Fourteen: Beyond Generosity

131   Chapter Fifteen: Beyond Gethsemane

Introduction

Although there are goals we all want to achieve in life, and different approaches of achieving them, it is incredibly important that we do not confuse the goal with the journey we take to get there. If we aren't careful, the journey can take all of our attention, to the point where we never even reach our destination. This happens to a lot of people, and their goals remain forever out of reach.

The original generation lost sight of their goal, in the process of surviving the wilderness, and expired. The goal that God held out for them became obscured by the issues of their journey—their focus shifting from where they were going to how they were getting there. It's like focusing on following Jesus without realizing that He is actually *leading* you somewhere... and that at some point, you will actually arrive.

In the same way, we can put all our energy into obedience, making *it* the goal and destination. But obedience is a means to an ideal end, not the end in and of itself. Obedience is totally significant, but we cannot just park there as if it is where our journey was leading us all along. When we start seeing and thinking of obedience as the journey toward an ideal destiny, it puts an even greater importance on it. This book you are holding does not focus on emphasizing obedience though, since there are already great books and teaching materials out there on the subject. The intent of this book is to emphasize going *beyond* obedience... and what we can do, with God's help, to get there. Obedience is primarily the realm of one who has the status of a servant. And to be clear, we must always must retain the *attitude* and *heart* of servanthood, regardless what status we actually attain. But with servant status alone, commandment is required for obedience to be exercised. This is not a ruling status. Servants do not rule, nor do slaves. They are ruled by someone above or beyond their level. We will not change the world by serving it... but by ruling it with a servant's heart.

Jesus said to His disciples that He would not call them servants anymore, but friends. He shifted them to a higher status. For them to be co-labourers with Christ, He *had* to raise their status. In Deut. 22:10, God instructed His people that they should not plough with an ox and a donkey together. By this, He meant that, if a certain work is to be done, it must be done with compatible partners. By the same token, we cannot be co-labourers *with* Jesus while remaining in the status of a slave or servant. We must move into the kingship He arranged for us, so we can indeed be partners and co-labourers with Jesus the King.

Jesus makes kings out of slaves and servants so that we all can work in the kingdom of God. The enormous price Jesus paid was not simply for our past dues. He purchased royal status for us.

In Hebrews 5:8, scripture says that Jesus, as the son of God, learned obedience by what He experienced. His life served to teach us that, in the status of a servant, we learn the heart and ways of our master. The purpose of such learning is to prepare us for ultimately ruling and reigning in His kingdom. At some point, we must graduate from servanthood to leadership.

Obedience should never be applied as a cure for rebellion. Jesus was not rebellious, but He learned obedience through the experiences of submission to the Father. Rebellion is as the sin of witchcraft. Rebellious people do not obey. Forced obedience does not cure a rebellious spirit. Deliverance by the Holy Spirit's power is what sets the rebellious free.

Obedience must be redeemed to its noble purpose. When obedience is used as punishment for rebellion, it gives obedience a negative view that it does not deserve or warrant. Obedience is the only path that qualifies us for advancement into leadership. Those who strive for and attain leadership, without the qualification of an attitude of servanthood, are dangerous people indeed.

Emphasizing kingship does not depreciate the realm of obedience. It actually puts more significance and importance on the status of servanthood, as a necessary predecessor to leadership. However, we do not want to stop short of what God has intended for us.

Phil. 2:5 – 11 gives us a revelation of the merits of obedience. Jesus' obedience qualified Him for His Father's exaltation of Him. While on earth, Jesus took on the status of a servant for three and half years. But Jesus did not stay in this status. Presently, all power and authority is given to Him as He is positioned at the right hand of the Father. At some point, He graduated from servant status to kingship status.

Gal. 4: 1, 2 teaches this concept also. Though one may be an heir, as long as he is still under development, and yet to learn obedience, he does not experience ruling over his rightful inheritance. It is necessary for such a one to be subject to the school of obedience. When that is successfully completed, one experiences what once was only positional.

The attitude of a servant must remain constant, regardless what status we advance to. Our need to graduate to leadership is for the purpose of serving the world more effectively. Christ's kingship must be transmitted to this world if any substantial changes for good are to occur. When rulership is corrupt, self-serving, advantage-taking, and self-exalting, the entire global society suffers.

There is plenty of everything for everybody in the world. Poverty and lack is not necessary at all. There is more than enough food, shelter, education, and means for health. Corruption has made it unreachable and unaffordable by distorting distribution. The love of money by those in charge creates the unnecessary evil. Certain evil systems keep their subjects in lack and poverty just to keep them voiceless and subject to their dictatorships. Godly leadership is the most critical need in our present chaotic world.

Believers across the entire world, and in all aspects of our society, must do more than humbly serve while ungodly systems produce chaos by their ungodly rulership. It's not enough to deal with lack and poverty. We must deal with what is producing it. When the Godly are in authority, the people rejoice. When the wicked bear rule, the people mourn (Prov. 29:2). We must take certain initiatives to move beyond being servants only and learn to rule.

Salvation is activated when we take initiative and confess Jesus as Lord. The transforming power of God is put into action by the initiative we take. This is how it all starts, this is how it continues, and this is how it advances. We do have a role to play in ushering in God's kingdom. God will not impose himself on us with His kingdom; there is certain 'action' you can take.

God desired this for Israel many years ago. The possession and retention of the promise required more than the concepts of the slave or servant status experienced in Egypt. It required a transition—a shift from one status to another in order to conquer and possess what God promised them. When Israel lost the promise, it was because they failed in their rulership... not in their servanthood.

God always delivered His people from captivity. God did not call His people to bow to any system or being except Jesus Christ. Their deliverance was from being a slave or servant to rulership in the land of promise. Obedience is the learning time for graduation to rulership. We too need to be delivered from our bondage mentality and move into kingship thinking.

In Exodus 19:5, 6, God said that, if God's people were first obedient, they would become kings and priests unto God. 1 Peter 2:9–10 says we are a royal priesthood. Rev. 1:5, 6 declares Jesus made us kings and priests unto our God. Along with numerous other such like scriptures, it is evident the Lord wants us to rule and reign with Him in His kingdom. Being that His kingdom is eternal, it means we can experience and exercise that rule now.

Kingdom rule needs to be first experienced in our personal lives. Many of our troubles are due to the fact that the Holy Spirit did not rule as Lord in our lives. The repetitive deliverances we continue to seek are caused only by the lack of ruling and reigning. We need to retain our breakthroughs and walk in the power of Jesus' Lordship. Without ruling, we slip back into the same bondage over and over again.

Jesus did mighty works of God by His authority. The rulers of that day were not as impressed with what He did, but were taken back by how He did it. They recognized that He was more than a gifted healer, a powerful deliverer, or a typical miracle worker. They recognized that He did all this with authority. Deliverance can get us out of bondage, but only authority can get us out of bondage and keep us out.

God's people need to move into the rulership God has provided through Jesus Christ. Rule your passions, lusts, sins, thinking, time, priorities, energies, and ministries—the list can go on and on, covering our whole life. We will never rule a city or the world if we have not perfected rule in our own life. We can and (according to Jesus Christ's sure plan for us) we will. We have Christ the King in us. Let Him rule.

Chapter One

What time is it?

GOD GAVE ME the most wonderful in-laws a son-in-law could hope for. They were people who prayed for us daily. Their confession of love for Jesus matched their work with Him. God blessed us with having them for many years before they graduated to heaven.

We took advantage of occasions and events to just be together with them. It was always a great blessing to get together and enjoy one another's company. They were up-to-date about what God was doing around the world. It was a house of fellowship, prayer, laughter, and the awesome warmth of God's love.

It was my in-laws' wedding anniversary again. With each passing year, it became more and more challenging to buy them a gift, whether it was for their birthdays, Christmas, or (in this case) an anniversary. By now there was not much they needed. Any gift we gave them had to be very useful and practical, otherwise they made it very clear that we were wasting our money. They were very generous when it came to giving to the church and others, but were very frugal when it came to spending money on themselves.

Well, this time we felt we had been incredibly successful, buying them what we thought was a practical but unique gift. It was a bird clock—unique indeed and on major discount. At the strike of every hour, a different bird chirped. It was not necessary to see the clock; night or day, one always knew what time it was. We were so excited to present our unique find to our wonderful parents on this their special day. They hung the clock on the living room wall of their old quaint house. It did not take more than a few days to know what the time was by which bird chirped or sang. We were totally unaware of the possibility that the mechanism could wear out sooner than we anticipated. After only a few weeks, the birds all began to sound as though they had a horrible case of laryngitis.

While we were having tea and cake in their house, the serene country atmosphere was suddenly shattered. It was the screech owl's turn to announce a new hour. Owls do not sound pleasant at the best of times, but this was exceptionally irritating. It reminded me of the old chalk board at school and how, as kids, we would scrape our fingernails across it.

Perhaps this was the reason why the price of the clock was discounted, with red words stamped on the tag: "Final sale!"

The next time we visited the parents, the clock and the twelve birds had migrated from the house to the work shop. There, in obscurity, the gargling, screeching, choking birds would live out their last days disturbing no one. The work shop was a sort of hospice for anything that mother did not happily appreciate in the house.

We knew the process. In a short while, the clock would show up in our own treasure chest as an early inheritance. From our house, we would let the birds and clock migrate to a yard sale. There was no telling where those birds would eventually end up. We were just happy they did not return the following spring.

Regardless how irritating the bird clock sounded, as long as the clock was in the house, we had known what hour it was, which put me in mind of something: Among the many other great reasons for King David's success was his respect for the ministry of the tribe of Issachar. They were gifted by God to be able to tell Israel of the times there were in and how to respond.

One day Jesus stood in a place where He could view the entire city of Jerusalem. He wept over it, because it was (at that significant moment in its history) missing the visitation of the Messiah. Jesus was not weeping for Himself. He was not feeling sorry for Himself, because they were not believing that He was the very One they were waiting for. Jesus wept for *them*.

They would miss the blessings of the salvation He came to give. All that the prophets prophesied, all the types and shadows of the Old Covenant now being fully fulfilled... they were missing it all. Not only missing it, but rejecting what and who they had been waiting for. Why? They rejected the voice of the prophets. They killed the prophets. The last such significant prophet was John the Baptist. He came in the spirit of Elijah and they ignored him. They took advantage of his water baptism but ignored his introducing the Messiah.

When the prophetic ingredient is not readily functioning in the church, we lose the spiritual reference point by which we are able to identify divine time and what to do. At that point, instead of hearing what the Holy Spirit is saying concerning our times, we revert to natural happenings, trying to read God's time clock. We who have the Spirit of God should not have to read natural events to tell time. That might be necessary for those who do not have the Spirit of God, but not for Spirit-filled and Spirit-led people.

Perhaps we need the irritating prophetic sound of a screech owl to wake us up—to spiritually disturb us from the comfort of our religious sleep. We do need to know that it is high time for Jesus' prayer to be answered. Jesus decreed that God's kingdom, which is in heaven, would come to earth. Evil forces know this and are outraged and anxiously expressing their hatred in extreme measures. The kingdom of darkness is in fear and panic. That is why there is such bizarre behaviour lately around the world.

God's kingdom is not limited to getting saved and being rushed off to heaven. It's a matter of bringing heaven to earth. God cares about this world. He is not writing it off. He would not have sent His only begotten son to pay such an incredible price for the whole world just to abandon it.

That is why Jesus made us kings and priests unto our God. Kings rule and reign. They do not stand around debating doctrine. We, as the salt and light of the world, are here to make a difference. God's plan is certain; we will rule and reign with Christ on earth. That ruling and reigning is by the same love that was demonstrated on Calvary. It's the same rule that makes heaven what it is. The last I heard, most want to go there.

It would be humorous if it was not so serious. Everyone wants to go to heaven where none of the systems we are willing to die for on earth operate. Would it not be sensible and easy to say with Jesus, "Thy kingdom come"? Why is humanity so stubborn about their own systems, which have brought war, strife, murder, poverty, slavery, and all such like results?

We would not keep fixing a car that never gets us to our destination. It would be traded for a better one. How come we are so committed to systems of government that we invented, even though they are not really working? These have been operated for years with very limited results.

Why has all this been said? It is because God is saying to today's church that it's time for a shift. The shift is to graduate us from the status of servanthood to kingship. Much has been taught about servanthood. That is not to be ignored or disrespected. However, Christ did not expect us to stay at that level. Jesus said to His disciples, 'I call you no more servants but friends.'

Wow. Do you know what that implies? It implies being a part of the community of equals.

Of course, no one would be as foolish as Lucifer to exalt themselves to be equal with God. However, Christ made us kings. God made us in His Likeness... created us in His image. We are born of the Holy Ghost; we are His offspring, sons and daughters, and that is bigger than is presently comprehended.

We are filled with the Holy Spirit, we have Christ in us, and we are born by the Word of God. Jesus said, 'Go do the works that I do and greater.' Jesus said, 'As I am in the world, so are you.' We are co-labourers with Christ, heirs of God, and God is our Father. Is this going to be the generation that gets this?

It is time to wake up and embrace the status Christ has given us. The cross did not just pay for what we owed; it purchased a status for us in Jesus Christ. We celebrate the payment for our sins but need to glory in what Christ has purchased for us.

Jesus said, 'I give you power and authority over all the power of the devil and diseases.' Yet listen to our prayers. We are still asking Jesus to do what He told *us* to do. Jesus said, 'Heal the sick.' But we are afraid of our own shadows and pray for Jesus to heal people.

The Bible teaches that we are privileged to partner with Jesus in the establishment and proclamation of His kingdom. Jesus said that it was the Father's good pleasure to give us the kingdom. Through divine birth, we have entered into our Father's kingdom.

In Old Covenant times, Moses spoke and Egypt was dealt with. Joshua spoke and the sun and moon stood still. Elijah spoke and it did not rain. He spoke again and it rained. The Roman Centurion said to Jesus, 'Just speak the word and my servant will be healed.' This faith Jesus marvelled at. Now remember, all these were before the time of the cross. All these were in a lesser covenant. Now we have a greater and better covenant. Why do we put up with such a limited Christian experience?

We let the heathen rule God's world, while we have our little religious devotionals. The Bible is not a devotional book; it is the LAW book of the kingdom of God. It is a book of covenants, laws, commandments, ordinances, judgements, thrones, kings, and judges. The Almighty God is the lawgiver and eternal judge. The Holy Spirit is our advocate. We have an everlasting representative and intercessor, Jesus Christ.

That does not sound like a devotional but a law office—the throne of heaven and earth.

All areas of our lives and ministry will experience a shift when we fully embrace who Christ has made us. Our prayers will do less begging and pleading as a servant would and do, and more declaring and decreeing like a king. We will learn that we can send His word and heal what needs to be healed in our house. Remember Jesus is the Lord of lords, not the Lord of slaves. Jesus is the King of kings, not the King of servants.

The kingdom of darkness is not threatened because we are blessed. It is threatened when we really have a greater revelation of who God has made us to be in Jesus. What we have does not give us authority; it's who we are in Him that does.

Lucifer violated the throne of God in heaven and got evicted. He only said in his heart—things contrary to the rulership of God—and was immediately removed. When Jesus says, 'Pray that God's will be done on earth as it is in heaven, and that the heavenly kingdom come to earth,' Satan knows what that means for him on earth. It means ultimate eviction. Satan's stress concerns the believers' authority... not the believers' blessings.

God fully intended the righteous to rule. His will and purpose will certainly come to pass. Believers must shift to a ruling mentality, rather than one of escapism. The earth is the Lord's and the fullness thereof. It does not belong to the kingdom of darkness and its agents. We do have a role to play and a responsibility to make the shift from servanthood status to kingship.

Chapter Two

Beyond Obedience

IN THE LAST era of Christendom, we have primarily focused on the priesthood of the believer. Though there has been some emphasis on the kingship of the believer, in scattered pockets of Christianity, it now is becoming more intensified. Revivals and refreshings of the Holy Spirit have enhanced and restored our relationship with Christ. Communion with Jesus is totally critical to the health of kingdom life. Fellowship with Christ must ever increase.

Being that Christianity is not just another religion, but the manifest kingdom of heaven, the dimension of kingship in the believer's life is significant. The status of being a servant is a season of learning. At some point, we must advance and graduate to the status of kingship for a more empowered ability and right to serve. God wants to position His people so that they can serve the world from the top down. That is the most effective way to bless the world with the peace Jesus as King came to give.

Above all the things Jesus is and came to be in the world, He affirmed and declared His Kingship. (John 18: 33-39) He indeed is the King of kings and the Lord of lords. (Rev. 17:14). He also made us like Him, priests and kings unto our God. (Rev 5:10). This is the kingdom Jesus came to establish on earth. (Matt. 6:10)

Only then will the crimes of humanity cease. Bloodshed, retaliation, discrimination, radical destructive belief systems, terrorism, and all such like will be overcome with a Christ-like nature and character. Nothing can effectively and permanently change until the heart of man is transformed by the power and love of the Holy Spirit.

God will not, and indeed cannot in good conscience, give the power of rulership to an untransformed rulership. It would be like letting a child drive a high-powered sports car. Such an act would be unwise and destructive. Power and authority must equally correspond with maturity of character, which are increasingly sourced in Christ. Anything short of this explains the dilemmas we are all facing at every sector and level of our global society.

Dictators, corrupt leaders, and self-serving rulers are devoid of the character of Christ. Authority and power is dangerous and destructive without a nature sourced and sustained in Christ Jesus. All rulership must be based on the experiential knowledge of Christ. True leadership is governed and empowered by the Lordship of the Holy Spirit. Unless Jesus is Lord in our lives, governments, philosophies, and the world will simply keep degenerating, like meat without salt to preserve it.

Jesus Christ is the only one and true source of reproducing the kind of leadership God created the world for. He does not reproduce slaves to lead His wonderful world or dictators to manipulate it for their own uncontrolled lusts and passions. The date on God's calendar is fast approaching when all this human nonsense will end.

Ruling systems that promise to do everything for their subjects lure them into ultimate dictatorship and control, enslaving their subjects. The more responsibility we relinquish, the more control we hand over to the advantage takers. When we refuse to advance in the authority of the kingship Jesus intended for His people, we create a climate in which dictators emerge.

When Jesus instructed us to follow Him, He was leading us somewhere with a purpose. At some point, Jesus wants us to walk *with* Him, not *behind* Him. That is the point when we graduate from the status of servant to the status of kingship. We become co-labourers with Him—partners in the rulership and blessing of His kingdom.

Jesus prayed a prayer that He wants us to actually respond to, not just pray. In Matthew 6:10, Jesus declared for God's will, which is done in heaven, to be done in earth. He also prayed and invoked the kingdom of God to come to earth. Even a quick glance at the prayer tells us that Jesus prayed for something so great that only God's Spirit could help us comprehend it.

In the book of Revelation, Rev. 11:15, a final conclusion is stated. The kingdoms of this world will become the kingdoms of the Lord and of His Christ. This is a statement of fact by the Lord Himself and will certainly come to pass. Heaven will rule this earth as God intended in the original plan.

The intent of this material is to inspire us to move beyond where we are or have been for a long time. Actually, the ball is in our court. God is waiting on us to make the move. God is very ready to respond to your fresh Godly initiative.

Chapter Three

Beyond Request

A COLD BLAST OF arctic air introduced the first day of a long Canadian prairie winter. The snow came down like confetti at a wedding. The cold north wind sifted the snow across the frozen ground, swirling it around every object in its path. Soon the fields looked like a snapshot of ocean waves, as mounds of snow were building up everywhere.

As evening arrived, a poor but happy family snuggled in for the night in their old house. The house's poor insulation and single window panes were no match for this blistery arrival. Nor was the fire in the old stove any match for the ever plunging mercury.

No improvements were done to compete with this weather, since finances were a challenge for the family. The crackling fireplace produced more psychological comfort than heat. As the family was about to retire for the night, still savouring their hot chocolate with a story and a prayer, somebody knocked on the door.

It startled and surprised the family. No one could imagine getting company this late at night, especially in this storm. All held their breath as the father went to the door. As he opened it, a stranger apologized for coming to their door so late, but said he could explain. The father invited him in from the cold, and he joined the family at the kitchen table.

After a brief introduction, the man told them that he was in the area to do some big game hunting. Before he could ask if he could possibly lodge there for a few days, the father offered it to him. Being a very hospitable family, payment was not even discussed. After a hot cup of tea, arrangements were made to accommodate the man.

Unbeknownst to the father, this man had already stopped at a few of their neighbours' homes, hoping to get room and board. He was denied. Maybe it was because he was unshaven, dressed very casually, and had a one-owner four by four, which desperately needed some major cosmetic attention. In any case, a private room was arranged for him, as the kids crashed on their parents' bedroom floor. He felt so bad inconveniencing the family. Though he offered to sleep in his sleeping bag on the old couch, the family would not hear of it.

The father got the house fires roaring first thing in the morning, while mother made a generous country breakfast for everyone. She made the children's school lunches and a special lunch for the hunter to take with him. The children scrambled on foot to their country school just half a mile away. The stranger drove off toward the forest to hunt.

It only took a few days for the hunter secured his game. *to secure* Since the family refused to take the money he offered, he gave them some of the meat in appreciation. He was more interested in the moose head and massive rack of antlers than the meat. He gave each of the children some candy money and left for home.

In this tight-knit community, it was not long before everyone knew that this family had taken the stranger in. They all boasted about how they had refused to host him, since he looked a bit questionable. After all, no one wanted to be inconvenienced with a stranger's need.

The small town coffee shop was buzzing with criticism, ridiculing the family for what they had done. They asked why this man would help a stranger for free when he did not even have enough for his family. The grocery man knew how little food they could afford. The local mechanic shop knew they couldn't even afford to winterize their old car. The children's teacher chimed in, describing how poorly the children were dressed, especially for such cold days.

A number of weeks went by. Christmas arrived and with it came a Christmas card to the old house. It was from the stranger. He wrote gracious words of appreciation. Included in the card was another sealed envelope. In a brief note he told them that, when he was leaving the area, he had stopped at the one and only bank in the village and deposited some money into their account.

In this envelope, he left suggestions for what to do with the money: buy clothing for the children, groceries for the house, and a reliable vehicle, and in the spring "build yourself a nice four-bedroom home. When I come back in the fall for hunting, I'd like to stay in that fourth bedroom. Merry Christmas and indeed have a happy new year."

Wow, can you imagine the chatter in the coffee shop now! Some believed it, others doubled over in laughter, and still others were now willing to host the stranger they had turned away. But it was too late. Opportunity knocks on our door only once.

Opportunities usually come packaged in the ordinary and common. They come when we least expect them. They arrive at our door at the wrong time of day, when we are unprepared, too busy, too tired, and unwilling to sacrifice. The father did not wait to be asked to host this man. He willingly took initiative and offered his house to him. He did not have much but shared what little he had. No one imposed themselves on him, nor begged. He did not expect a reward or pay. He made no excuses but responded with a pure motive. Do not wait for a command; be a leader and go beyond just obedience.

Chapter Four

Beyond Telling

A MOTHER ASKED HER son to take the trash out to the curb for the city to collect it. Without hesitation the young lad responded. Many parents could only wish their children were that obedient. This boy learned obedience from an early age.

Before the mother realized, the boy grew up to become a fine young man. He was now taking courses at the local university and still living at home. He was a blessing to his single mother and always willing and obedient. Whatever his mother told him to do, he ungrudgingly did it.

One particular morning the young man was late for his class. As he was rushing out the door, his mother asked him to take the trash can to the curb for the city to pick up. His books in one arm, the trash can in the other, he dashed out the door.

He ran across the shaggy lawn, jumping over the tangled hoses left from summer watering. He joined other students on their way to the same university. This all appeared very well but something was missing and overlooked.

When he returned home that evening, for a brief moment he thought that he was at the wrong address. The lawn was mowed and the hoses were neatly rolled up and put away. The hedges were trimmed and the entire yard was manicured neatly. He knew no one else could have done this, except his busy mother. As the young man hurriedly entered the house, he saw his mother busily preparing for what appeared to be a large dinner. Unexpected company was due to arrive that evening. Feeling badly about his weary mother having to do all that yard work, he said something that indicated his level of maturity.

The young man said to his mother that she should have told him to mow the lawn, trim the hedges, and neatly store away the hoses. He emphasized his concern again and again. "Just tell me and I will obey." He really meant it. He was totally sincere. All he said was right... but incomplete.

At that age, why did his mother have to tell him what he should have already known to do? How come he never graduated from needing to be told? He was obedient but had not matured beyond it. He took no initiative to do what needed doing without being told.

The young man was still in the mode of needing to be told before he did anything. This is the status of a servant, not a leader. He was still operating in the command and obedience mode. This is acceptable for a growing child but not for an adult.

Why didn't this young man mow the lawn, put away the hoses, trim the hedge, vacuum the floors, dust the furniture, and do whatever else needed to be done? Simple. He was not asked to it or told to do it. Unless this young man gets weaned from needing to be told what to do, his success as a future leader will be compromised.

Salvation has been fully provided for us by Jesus Christ. A decisive act of faith is required to repent, confess, and believe in initiating salvation. We cannot be forced or commanded to confess Jesus as Lord and Saviour. We must take personal initiative and act on the gospel message.

Christ also provided kingship for us to enter into. Like in salvation, there is certain initiative we must take to shift from our beginnings as a servant to the leadership Christ desires for us. We will not be commanded or told to make this shift. It's totally up to us to make that call.

Chapter Five

Beyond Basic Labour

HAVE YOU WORKED and worked, hoping to get that ever elusive promotion? You have waited for it so long. You did what you were told, always on time and never leaving early. By now, you are struggling with an attitude of disappointment, especially when your co-workers get advances either in pay or position.

Sometimes it is possible to have an inconsiderate boss who is unfair and takes advantage of the diligent. In other words, it would not matter how wonderful a worker would be, favour would not be granted. Read this material carefully and prayerfully and try for promotion one more time. After that, look for a new boss. Do not get stuck being enslaved to a single level. Move on to new challenges where you will be appreciated and promoted.

The account recorded in Luke 17: 7-10 is challenging to understand. Since I was a youth, I had trouble grasping the truth concealed in this unique story told by Jesus. The way the master in this particular story was treating his employee always seemed unfair to me. I avoided preaching from its text for many years.

In this story, Jesus said that this servant laboured hard all day, taking care of the master's fields and cattle. After a long weary day, the servant returns home. He first attends to all his master's needs. He ignores his own need for food and rest. One would think any boss would be thrilled with a servant like this. Not this master.

The master did not think this servant was even worthy to be thanked. Even more disturbing than that, he called him an unprofitable servant. This is what really stunned me for years, because I could not understand the master's attitude. The end of this account states the reason the master felt this way about this servant.

The Bible says this servant did only what he was told to do. He obeyed all the commands. He followed all the instruction precisely. All that was expected of him he did and no more. He had his job description down perfectly. So why was he considered unprofitable to the master's empire?

Simple. He still required supervision and verbal direction. He did not do what he (by now) knew was the right thing to do. There was no motivation to go beyond the command.

Great obedience but nothing beyond that. It cost the business to have this servant work there, because he still needed to be administrated. Such workers cost more to maintain than what profits they create for the company.

In this story, the servant will remain in this limited status for a long time. Until he becomes aggressive and learns the heart of the master, he will not experience promotion. A potential leader learns what is required while under command and obedience mode, but he does not stay in that status. He takes initiative and acts on the knowledge and experience he has concerning the master's business. This is what sets him up for a promotion.

The Bible says, in Rev. 11:15, that the kingdoms of this world will become the kingdoms of the Lord and of His Christ, who will reign forever. This is the ultimate goal the Lord has for the world. For this to be possible, and it *will* become possible, leadership is required. The kingdom of God needs people with initiative and a leadership mentality. Those who go beyond the call of duty qualify themselves to transition from being a servant to a leader. We will indeed rule and reign with Him. Let's get ready.

Chapter Six

Beyond One Talent

A WEALTHY MASTER PLANNED a lengthy business trip far away. He called his three best servants and entrusted them with various portions of his money. What each of them decided to do with this money would determine their future status in the 'the master's kingdom'. But the master did not inform the three servants of what his intentions were for trusting them with so much money. They were not aware that this was a test for promotion—from servants to leaders.

Evidently, the business was doing very well. The master needed more leaders to run his empire, and not only servants. Being a successful man himself, the master understood that those who are leaders are self-starters. These people do not need to be told what to do; they evaluate what needs to be done and do it. A leader who progresses from a servant position exercises self-motivation. He does not wait for commands. He pre-obeys a command yet unuttered. This is what graduates one from a labourer to a leader in some capacity.

The three servants the master chose were his very best. He could trust them with large sums of money. They qualified themselves by being consistently obedient to all the master's commands. They displayed a character worthy of trust. The master had certainly observed them for a long time while they served as servants. But now he needed more leaders.

When all three were given their portions of money, the master left, giving no instructions as to what they should do with it. Nor was there any opportunity to contact him and ask for guidance.

Until now, as servants, they operated by command and instruction. They were totally unaware that they were being weaned from that mode of function. Now they would need to think for themselves as to what to do with the master's money. Decisions would need to be made and accountability given. Hiding in the shadows of a leader and looking good was not an option. What was challenging was that none of them were aware that they were being tested for graduation to a leadership status.

There is a very powerful truth here. When you wait and wait for God to speak to you and all you get is silence, it may be more of a blessing than you think. God may not be ignoring you at all but rather giving you an opportunity to advance from a servant to a ruler. His silence to your request is actually Him saying, "You know what to do; I trust you with it. Just do it and I will bless you and promote you as a leader."

If the Lord speaks instruction to you, it will keep you in the status of a servant. Servants do what they are told; kings make decisions and take actions. God is not ignoring you when you feel that heaven is brass. He is giving you an opportunity to take initiative and act without being told. This is what will catapult you into your next status. God has a lot of servants in His kingdom, but there is a shortage of leaders. In fact, it is God's will that all be leaders in their own sphere of life and responsibility.

There are those who wait for something to happen, and there are others who make it happen. Some wait to be told, administrated, and supervised. Some want a job to look for them instead of looking for a job. These people are still in a servanthood status mentality. They can decide either to stay there or take initiative and do something about it.

After a lengthy absence, the master returned. The three servants were called to give an account of how they had managed the talents. This time it was not an accountability of their obedience but of their motivation. Times before, as servants, they would just check off a "to do" list. Not this time. There was no list. They had to come up with their own "to do" list as leaders and not as followers.

When it seems like the master has absented himself from you, it means he trusts you with making a decision. Jesus did not give us potentials, callings, gifts, and awesome abilities to enslave us by them. The master in this story gave such major portions of his money to these servants because he trusted them. He did not want them to see themselves as servants who still needed detailed instruction to accomplish something. The master needed these three to graduate from that and become the rulers he saw them to be.

The servant with the five talents and the other with the two talents both doubled the master's money. They did not sit around waiting for somebody to tell them what to do. They took risks, invested, and stepped out of their usual servanthood mode. They were successful. Both were promoted to rulership. They would never regress to a servanthood status again. These two experienced obedience and now have gone beyond obedience to a kingship status.

The servant with one talent was called to give an accounting of how he had handled his portion. All he had were excuses as to why he did not double his talent. He did the typical thing, blaming others for his own defeats. He attacked his master's character, which was interesting because this was the master he'd chosen to be faithful to for many years.

Why make an issue of his perceived character flaw now? Why did this servant have such a negative attitude toward the boss he'd once loved? Why was this man so unmotivated to invest the talent and please the master? When the servant could not explain away why he had not doubled his talent, the master punished him severely, taking away not only his opportunity for promotion but his original position as servant as well.

At this point we need a quick review of this servant. Why did he fail so miserably when the master had set him up for success? He was handpicked as one of the three best servants. There was something the master saw in this servant that the servant did not see in himself. He was actually picked for rulership. There was no error in the master's well processed judgement of this servant's potential. So what changed this servant's attitude toward his master, whom he had served faithfully for so long? How could he become all that the master said of him so quickly? Why was the punishment so severe? One would think that if one failed the test for leadership, you could just go back to be a servant. But that is not the case.

When the challenge to advance presents itself to us, we must do something about it. If we embrace it, we will advance. If we do not, we cannot just go back to where we were. That is a real challenging situation. The servant with the one talent, who failed to be advanced, could not go back and resume being a servant. That was eliminated by the punishment he received.

Once Israel left their place of bondage, they could not return. It seems that when God processes advancement in our lives, we cannot return to our past. The future must be embraced.

The Ark of the Covenant, at a certain point, was removed from Moses' Tabernacle. The manner by which the Ark was removed was negative. However, in the ultimate process, the Ark was placed in a new tabernacle: the Tabernacle of David. This ushered in a new day and a new way of worship and response to the Ark of the Covenant. Actually it was a New Testament manifestation in Old Covenant times.

I want to share a quick nugget of truth. When things are removed from our lives, even negativity, God always has something better and greater for our lives. Israel had a rough start; Joseph went through a painful process before they (and many like them) advanced in God's destiny. Be encouraged when changes come, and follow the Lord closely; He is leading you into a greater pasture. The old has to be done away with to make room for the new. Nothing is planned by God to go backwards to its former glory. The Holy Spirit moves only forward. When David was anointed to be the new king of Israel, God's spirit left Saul and his system of government, never to return, and then moved to David.

The reason there is no option to return to the past and enjoy it is because of God's loving and determined desire to see us advance into the fullness of His glory. Going back means the Spirit of life is no longer present. That is the reason past structures deteriorate and collapse. Going forward may be difficult at times but going back is certain spiritual death.

In order for one to be successful in cleaving, there first has to be a successful leaving. Inadequate leaving hinders the success of cleaving. This servant consented to the advancement and test for a new day. Failing did not just revert him to servanthood but actually to punishment and slavery. What really could have happened to this servant's attitude that such a horrific digression occurred in his life?

I believe there was a major misunderstanding in regards to why the servant received only one talent while his buddies got more. The servant took it as an insult against his character and ability. He misread his master's intention. He concluded that, after all the years of being faithful, he was not as trusted as the others. This embarrassed him among his peers, friends, and family. A root of bitterness developed deep in his soul.

Bitterness and anger changed this formerly great servant's character. He became very angry toward his master. It immobilized his ability to do the right thing with the one talent. He retaliated and hid the talent. Misunderstanding, a lack of forgiveness, and bitterness will definitely keep us from doing the right things and graduating to a new day. The master he once loved and served, he now hated.

There is a message of caution in this man's experience. Do not resist what God intends for you, to run you into your next experience. Do not fight the wind, which was planned to make you fly higher. Where the doors are locked, that is where the treasure is. Turn your stumbling stones into stepping stones. A good seed will use all the dirt and fertilizer thrown at it.

Esau ran Jacob into a place that he called Bethel, the house of God—a place where angels ascended and descended. This was where God choose to dwell and communicate. Not bad for a get-away from an angry brother. Jacob would have never experienced this glory and revolutionizing change from manipulator to prince if he would have chosen to fight with his brother.

Pharaoh ran Moses into exile, where he experienced God face to face numerous times. He became a mighty deliverer of God's people out of slavery, poverty, and bondage.

Joseph's brethren eventually ran him from a place of famine and mere existence to the plenteousness of the palace. If he would have chosen to be bitter, fight, or retaliate, God would not have promoted him to such glory. Jesus can still be your shepherd, even when you are on the run. He is too big to miss. You will run into Him.

If the servant with the one talent would have dealt with his offence, he could have been as successful as his friends, or even more so. It's not how much we have that determines our success. It's our attitude toward our master, Jesus Christ. A right attitude engages us with the one who can make something out of nothing, and take a little making it much.

So very many people feel they have been short changed in some way or area in their life. They see others seemingly favoured a lot more than they have been. The danger here is a tendency to develop the wrong attitude toward the Lord. If this is not corrected, a root of bitterness springs up in them, negatively affecting them and those they love. Let's get out of the box of offensive things and view this one-talent man from a possibility perspective.

The giving of only one talent to this servant was not meant as an insult but actually a compliment. The master saw such great potential in him that he knew he could accomplish more with one talent than the man with five. He had the ability to make ten or more talents with only one. Others required more to reach an intended goal. This one only needed a little to produce a lot.

Miracles are not performed with much but with very little. Otherwise it would not require a miracle. When there is only an impossible little, the God of all possibilities is attracted to it. The Lord always made a lot out of little. He never needed much to do a lot.

We all know about the multiplication of the widows little bit of meal and oil. What about the other widow's little bit of oil, which filled all the vessels from her neighbourhood and was still running? The loaves and fishes, that's something big from so little. Is our God still the same as He always was?

Jesus is saying to all of us that we are never limited with how little we receive. We are limited when we get the wrong attitude. We may only sow a tiny seed, but the God of all increase multiplies it into a net-breaking, bin-bursting, measure-overflowing harvest. Do not wait for faith the size of a mountain to overcome a mustard seed.

There are those who have been given so much but do so little. Others, who are blessed with so little, do so much. You may be that person feeling cheated because others got big opportunities, talents, and money, while you feel you received so little. Take that little and move a big mountain. Take that little pebble and kill a giant in your life. Take the little lunch into a crowd of hungry people, find Jesus, and feed the multitudes. It's not what you have, it's what He has that counts.

Offences are very damaging when not exposed, confessed, and dealt with properly. Bitterness and a lack of forgiveness will cripple divine potential in our lives. This servant with one talent did not have an ability problem. He had an attitude problem. It paralysed his God-given potential. Even if he would have been given five talents, his attitude would have spoilt it all.

Maybe you are waiting for a truckload of apples while ignoring the seed in your hand, with which you could create an orchard—like Elijah's servant, who had to go out and check the parched sky for a rain cloud seven times. Why seven times? Because he did not think such a little cloud could meet such a great need. He did not realize that the little cloud escorts the big one. When he reported what he thought was too small to be reportable, the entire sky turned into a rain cloud. The little may have been only of local potential, but when acknowledged and reported, it became a national impact!

Do not become intimidated with those who seem to have so much. Do not become jealous of them. It will demobilize your faith to act, to give, to invest, and to experience increase. Who said double was good enough? Break the mold of such limitations and believe your one talent can become a thousand. Do not hide in the shadows and be intimidated because you concluded you do not have much to offer. Do not insult the Master's high expectation of you. He believes you can do more with little than some others with much.

Quickly, go and dig up the talent you suppressed. Remove all excuses and reasons why it did not work for you. Think up reasons for how it can work, not why it can't. Quit blaming God and others. Be big enough to take responsibility squarely on your own shoulders. Wipe all self-pity tears away and envision a new day. Deal with bitterness toward your master. Admit it! Some have even convinced themselves that they are not offended with God. All of us are very good at that, but it's wrong. Your potential will sky rocket as soon as you confess, repent, and begin to experience the success awaiting for you.

Chapter Seven

Beyond Healing

TEN LEPERS, ISOLATED by their disease, cried out, "Unclean! Unclean! Unclean!" Their degenerating condition was painful enough to bear without having to confess it to everyone who came near them. Food and supplies were placed at a distance by their families and friends. All would stand far off. No hugs, no kisses, no embracing, just lonely isolation with those in the same condition. Emotionally numb, they just waited hopelessly for death to ultimately release them from this hell.

It is impossible to imagine how the families of these lepers were affected. An empty chair at the dinner table, no good-night story or hug for the children at bedtime. What about eventual graduations, weddings, and other such like events? What did the children say when asked by their peers, where is your father? Being evasive would only last a while, but to tell the truth could isolate the children from their friends fearing they might catch the disease.

Jesus, very God in the flesh, had time and interest to hear the cry of the forsaken and isolated. What others avoided, Jesus' love invaded. Religion proper could not see itself leaving its imagined loftiness and descending to where the destitute were. They were too busy with their policies, politics, pomp and ceremony. They were making too much religious noise to hear the weak cries of the hurting. When Jesus read Isa. 61: 1-3 in their synagogue, it was such a foreign idea that all they could do was stare at Him.

As the law required, Jesus sent the lepers to show themselves to the priests. They all obeyed. On the way to the temple, their leprosy was totally healed. All the lepers were cleansed of the dreaded disease. What happened next is very significant. Their obedience to Jesus' command blessed them with the first level of healing.

It was necessary by the law to show yourself to the priest. After the process of examining the lepers, the priest determined they were free to go back into society. Do you ever wonder what the ten lepers told the synagogue about how they got healed? Did they tell the priests that Jesus of Nazareth healed them? I wonder what the synagogue's response was as they checked out the undeniable miracles. It's amazing how blinding religion can be. Religion did not

only resist what it disagreed with but also eventually cruci-
fied the very one who came to bless them.

Nine of the lepers hurried home to announce their miracle.
Whatever was left of their bodies, shattered relationships,
business, and careers, they were going to make the best of it.
They were happy and willing to settle with all the losses this
disease incurred. Just to be healed was as wonderful as they
thought it could ever be.

Jesus, in seeing one leper return to Him, asked him where
the other nine were. Only this one leper had taken time to
find Jesus and give Him thanks. Jesus had not been waiting
for them in order to receive thanks. He was waiting to give
them the rest of the miracle he had for them. They needed
restoration and healing beyond the basic stopping of the
disease in their bodies.

Obedience brought healing and stopped the disease from
further destruction of their bodies. But what the disease
had damaged needed to be restored. Body parts needed
to be restored and replaced, relationships, finances, jobs,
and careers needed restoration. The mental and emotional
trauma needed attention.

Jesus honoured this one leper who returned to give thanks.
No instruction was given to do this. This was something this
leper did without being commanded. It is evident that Jesus
rewarded him for it. Jesus decreed wholeness to him. This
would restore everything leprosy had directly or indirectly

taken away from this man and his family. This one leper went beyond the limitations of just obeying a command and tapped into abundance.

This one leper had everything made whole. He was healed of the disease, parts destroyed because of leprosy were restored. Emotions damaged by rejection, despair, isolation, and such like devastations were healed. Finances, family, friends, and future were all put back in place by the wholeness Jesus gave him. This is what Jesus wanted to do for all of them, but only one tapped into such glory. Why? He had taken initiative to do something beyond command and obedience and God favoured him.

This second level of blessings does not come as a result of obeying a command. It comes as a result of taking initiative without being told what to do. This leper was healed by obeying Jesus command but fully restored by taking unsolicited action. Jesus gave this one leper total wholeness in all areas of his life. He experienced miraculous completeness. All because, on his own, he decided to do something beyond the basic. The rest of the lepers settled for too little too soon!

I wonder if this account by Jesus reveals a condition in Christendom. Could it be that only one out of ten believers desires to have an experience with Jesus beyond the basic? Are ninety percent of Christians content to do just the minimum requirement? Is the larger part of Christianity happy with just enough to survive?

Are too many just willing to be told what to do and do it without thinking for themselves? If it is true that only a remnant want more, only a small number desire to advance, then perhaps we can understand why we gave away our right to rule in the world. I have said it before but must say it again: In an environment of slavery and servant mentality, dictators emerge.

Hearing a command and obeying it is wonderful, but that reveals the status of a servant. Christ urges us to become the kings He has made us by doing something beyond the basic. He is watching for such so that He can position them in kingdom leadership. All ten lepers were healed by obeying Jesus' command. Only one was made whole because of personal unsolicited initiative.

Jesus is the Lord of lords and King of kings. He is not the Lord of slaves; nor does He want us to be servants forever. The kingdom of our Lord requires kings to operate it. The last and greatest move of God is going to bring His kingdom into full force on the earth. He needs more than servants to do this with. He needs leaders.

Chapter Eight

Beyond the First Level

ELIJAH'S PROPHETIC MINISTRY was coming to a close. The nation could not be without another prophet at least his equal. That, at best, would be a major challenge. Who else could control the rain in the land? Who else could call fire from heaven? Who else was brave enough to challenge the king and silence Jezebel's false prophets? There were schools of prophets, but none were brave enough to submit an application.

The nation had become spiritually bankrupt, with impending judgement looming on its horizon. Israel's spiritual decline made the nation vulnerable to its surrounding neighbours. A litany of evil kings had plunged the nation into moral decay. Worship was corrupted by compromised sacrifices on disrespected altars. God's ordinances were not only violated but ignored and voided from leadership. Truth and justice were a rarity. In spite of Elijah's powerful ministry, the nation required a new level of the prophetic, not only to stay judgement but to be restored to its original level of glory.

The intensity of the kingdom of God is ever increasing, coming quickly into its full expression on the earth. Jesus is building His church. That is an absolute. Those who preach that the church has failed are in the wrong church, built by the wrong man. Neither heaven nor hell will prevent Jesus' building program from succeeding. Those who criticize the church need to know how the groom feels about His bride.

The emergence of God's kingdom in our day has also alerted the kingdom of darkness and all its agencies. We have already mentioned that the intensified persecution of the church and its values is a sure sign of just how nervous Satan is. In the Old Testament, when the enemies of the promise heard about the miraculous glory and power in Israel, they built walls, increased their armies and fortified themselves. This is happening in our world, first in the spirit realm and expressed in the natural sphere.

A lot is said in these days about needing a greater anointing or a double portion of anointing. Perhaps this makes believers strive for more when they already have all it takes to do more. It is an issue of a greater manifestation of what we already have. Many are praying for more from God but God is waiting to have more from *us*... so He can manifest more of Himself *through* us. Our lives must become more and more yielded and translucent so that the power of the Holy Spirit can manifest more fully through us.

While ministering around the country, Elijah noticed a young man ploughing the field with twelve yoke of oxen. He took his mantle and threw it on this young man, whose name was Elisha. Elisha immediately processed a shut down to what he was doing and prepared to follow Elijah.

What we want to notice about Elisha is his decisiveness and the way he took control as a leader. Elijah did not command Elisha to follow him. He made that decision on his own. He was not told to bid his family farewell, nor to kill the oxen and barbecue them with the wood off the ploughs. These were decisions Elisha made without anyone telling him to.

It is interesting to consider how Satan has lied about God's generals. God never called losers to minister in His kingdom. God called individuals who already had a powerful resume. Just because others did not think much of them did not mean that they were losers. At times those who God called did not even think much of themselves, because they listened to critics. But God always told them who they were.

Elijah found a successful man to replace himself. Sometimes in Christianity we think we can make princes out of toads. Jesus made sure that the disciples were more successful in their fishing than ever before He called them to follow Him. Jesus did not need people to follow Him because nothing else worked. Jesus made sure their nets were to full capacity with fish and their boats were sinking low with a great catch before He called them to be fishers of men.

I have heard people say, "Maybe I should go into the ministry, because nothing else is working in my life." Trust me, if this is the case, neither will the ministry work for you. If you are going to deny self, you must first have something to deny. If you are going to put it all on the altar, how big of an altar would you need? If you are going to sell all and give it away, how much would that be?

Get educated. Succeed in life. Become as successful as you can be. When God requires something of you, you will have something to give Him. When God calls you to leave all and follow Him, you'll have something to leave. Don't sit around waiting for God to call you; get busy. He won't call you until you are.

God called Noah to build a floating zoo. Noah was smart enough to engineer it and rich enough to pay for it. He was convincing enough to get plenty of help and have family buy into it. That is not a dumb leader.

God called Moses who was the most educated Hebrew in his day. Who could work for his in-laws for forty years and succeed. Who could convince two million relatives to follow him into the wilderness. Who could respond to God and cripple Egypt, convincing Pharaoh to release two million slaves from free labour. Moses was not a loser.

When God called Abraham, he was already wealthy. He had an army of three hundred men. Wherever he went, the area could not host him because he was so big in wealth and possessions. Abraham was a man of good choices and powerful decisions.

We could talk about David and his awesome qualifications for kingship. What about David's men? Check out their resumes before David incorporated them into his kingdom.

The disciples were not losers, as some people have made them out to be. Fishermen were major business people. Luke was a physician, Matthew had a government job, Judas was an accountant, and Apostle Paul was a Pharisee of the Pharisees. No, God did not call losers to the ministry. These were all people of dynamic initiative and purpose in life.

Elisha took personal and aggressive action to make it completely impossible to return to his past. No one will do this for you; it is up to you. Make no provision to give up. Even if you fail, fail forward. If you fall or collapse, fall forward.

The Red Sea will not part for us to return to where we were. Jordan will not roll back for us to get out of the promise but into it. As long as we entertain returning to whatever our Egypt is, we will not go forward but expire in the process.

Elisha burned every bridge that could lead him back to his past. He eventually got blessed with a double portion of God's anointing. Israel was more mindful about where they came from than where they were going. That generation failed to reach God's intent for them. The priests hung on to the Old Covenant and could not embrace the new. Jesus said that he who puts his hand to the plough and looks back is not worthy of the kingdom. Apostle Peter never did get rid of his fishing boat. When confusion came concerning the kingdom and Jesus, Peter found it easy to say, "I go fishing."

It's not just a bad past that we must leave behind in order to succeed. Elisha did not have a negative past. He had a good and successful past. Such a past is more difficult to leave than a negative past. Someone once said that, many times, it's the good that hinders us from the best. We all need to appreciate our great past, but at the same time, not allow it to hold us from a greater future.

On his way up, Elijah asked Elisha what he would want for being such a faithful servant. Elijah noticed Elisha was not interested in the schools of the prophets they had just passed by. He was willing to cross the Jordan with him without being promised anything. Elisha was also willing to deny other opportunities while still not presented with a new one.

The schools of the prophets stood on their observation deck, watching what would happen to Elijah and especially Elisha. Christendom is full of overly cautious ministries and churches watching to see what will happen with those who take daring initiatives to reach a new level in God. They might decide to join the next move of God, if it is safe to do so. But at this point of pioneering into a new move of God, they politely hold back, not wanting their polished doctrines to get tarnished. They were afraid their squeaky clean organizational vehicles could get muddied up while pioneering new trails for the kingdom.

There is no record that the students of the school of the prophets offered any help to Elijah and Elisha. They gave them no lunch to munch, no boat to float over Jordan, no helping hand to hold, just suspicion from their safe religious observation tower. It was too far below their prophetic dignity to get their lily white hands dirty with serving Elijah. After all, Elijah did not graduate from their school, so his credentials were in question. They were in a "do nothing, just wait and see" mode.

On the other side of Jordan was the landing pad for Elijah's heavenly limo. On the other side of Jordan was Elijah's ascension experience. On the other side of Jordan was Elisha's double portion of God's glory. Just like for Israel, the promise was on the other side of the Jordan.

Jordan separated the men from the boys. It separated the mediocre from the aggressive. The average was on this side of Jordan, while the spectacular was on the other. Either you took initiative to cross, or you settled on this side of Jordan where it was common and safe. It was your choice.

Metaphorically speaking, Jordan represents a baptism of death to self and resurrection to a new day. Jesus said that we cannot just decide to follow Him. There has to be self-denial and taking up our cross. Only then do we qualify, not only to follow but to embrace effectively the destination. Sowing a seed is important, having hands laid on us is significant, and being prophesied over is great, but none of these replace self-denial. Everyone has a Jordan to cross.

The challenge about Jordan is that you cannot see what is on the other side. Elijah did not promise Elisha anything. Neither do we see any real sense in going through our own Jordan. It indeed is a step of faith. When we are enticed with what great rewards we will get when we cross our Jordan, it circumvents faith and true self-denial. It think we preach too much about the benefits of accepting Christ. Maybe sinners do not need to be sold on the gospel message but to embrace it because of the Spirit's conviction.

There are certain requests which cannot be made till we cross our Jordan. Elijah asked Elisha what was burning on his heart on the other side of Jordan. There are certain privileges on the other side that are not available to us before we cross. It's a pure step of faith to cross and not be lured by certain anticipated benefits. If you are still motivated by benefits and blessings, you think you have crossed Jordan, but you haven't. Crossing Jordan is a total death to self and not a sales pitch of wonderful options.

As great as the prophet Elijah was, Elisha's request for a double portion took him back. Most moves of God have felt that it was the best and the last, thinking that was assuming we know all God has for us. We must conclude that we do not know the ultimate greatness God has for his Church. Every move is a contribution to the next. Every revival just compounds God's ever increasing greatness.

The next move of God is already surprising the last one. It is incorporating all that God has done alone with what God is doing. That's the double portion of Gods great anointing. It will not stop at double. Anywhere in the Bible, where there is a double there is unlimited multiplication. Adam had to become double in order to multiply the likeness and image of God. God created Eve to accomplish this.

What Elisha asked for has never happened before. It was not taught in the school of the prophets. Elijah did not coax Elisha to do this. This was sheer faith and divine aggression. The bottom line of all we said in this chapter is that Elisha took unsolicited initiative to do what he did. Absolutely no one told him to do it. He did not follow a command so he could obey it. He went beyond obedience and move into the conduct of a leader.

The school of the prophets watched as Elisha received Elijah's mantle. He came back to the Jordan where he had miraculously crossed over with Elijah. Taking the mantle, he smote the waters and the Jordan parted. Elisha came back to the other side to serve the nation with what he received from the Lord.

Elisha crossed the Jordan twice. Once to get more from the Lord, the second time to share it with the world. The temple veil was torn in two, so that what we receive in Christ in the Holy of Holies could be shared with the world. There is self-denial in experiencing more from God and self-denial in sharing it with the world. In both these dimensions Elisha was not commanded or manipulated. Elisha took initiative, exercised the free will God gave him, and did God's will. You must also make that decision on your own. God will not violate your will.

Chapter Nine

Beyond Winning

T HE STORY IN 2 Kings 13:14-19 highlights the importance of self-motivated initiative—action taken that exceeds what is commonly expected. It is a willingness to go beyond the basic requirement of what is commanded. This kind of mentality creates healthy and necessary margins of safety and abundance. For example, putting wide margins between victory and defeat, bondage and freedom, poverty and prosperity.

King Joash needed a major victory over his enemy, who was threatening God's people. An average basic defeat was not enough. Just moving the enemy back a little was temporary. He would always remain close enough to create uncertainty and insecurity. The space between the enemy and God's people was too marginal.

Elisha's prophetic ministry was coming to an end. He was very ill at this point. Joash was in a panic. Who else could possibly replace Elisha? It was critical to get a word from God immediately for two reasons. Elisha was dying and the enemy was too close for comfort.

Joash's relationship with Elisha should have developed him well enough to be able to hear from God. He became too dependent on the prophet. Many go from coast to coast to get a word from God through mighty ministries of various conferences. While we do this and are blessed, we must also develop a hearing ear to the voice of God. Joash could have tasted, prayed, and learned how to hear from God—including embracing Elisha's prophetic gift. Ideally, the five ministries mentioned in Eph. 4:11 are to develop the effectiveness of the saints in their own callings. Jesus said that it was profitable for us that He go away. When Jesus ascended to the Father, the Holy Spirit was sent to empower us to hear from God and have that supernatural power to fulfil Christ's will.

Elisha asked Joash to shoot an arrow out a window facing the enemy. Symbolically speaking, this act was to secure a certain level of victory over the enemy. It was a limited victory. It would not have a big enough margin to bring lengthy security for God's people. This type of victory was accomplished by Joash getting a command and precisely obeying that command.

The prophet expected more from Joash than just obeying a command. Joash was a king. Joash could make certain decisions as a king and they would be fulfilled. But instead, Joash reduced himself to the status of a servant, operating only on command. The king is supposed to take initiative and give commands, not be commanded. It was time for Joash to be a leader and not a follower.

Unknown to Joash, God arranged an occasion for him to exercise initiative beyond the basic expectation. Elisha asked the king to take an arrow and smite it on the ground. He was not told how many times to strike the ground with the arrow. The king's response would determine how complete his victory would be over his enemy. The king's aggression would be revealed in what he did with the arrow. How far would he determine to go beyond the basic command?

Joash took the arrow, striking the ground only three times. The prophet became angry with him. His unenthused effort revealed his lack of aggression toward the enemy. It revealed his casualness concerning the safety and security of God's people. He lacked passion and unstoppable determination. His concept was only a basic victory, not one that would make him more than a conqueror.

It is amazing that our aggression and determination is observed by the Lord. Not only is it observed, but our effort—our drive for God—determines how God responds on our behalf. Scripture is true. What we sow we reap. If we are laid back and casual about God, and about His kingdom, we will experience a casual shallow blessing. How often you sow, and how much you sow, certainly determines the size of your harvest.

Elisha told the king that his response only obtained a limited victory. The victory would not have a major margin between God's people and the enemy. All Joash would accomplish is suppression of the enemy, not possession of his gates. The entire nation was affected by a poor response of one man who had the authority to do much more. He only fulfilled a minimal requirement.

Let our expression of faith transcend minimal requirements. Worship and praise beyond what is the expected norm. Tithe and then show generosity in your offerings, beyond being *told* what to give God. Many wait for God to tell them what to give. How about we give without waiting to be told? You are a king made like unto God by Jesus Christ. Heaven is waiting for you to act like one.

Biblical history reveals that Joash experienced a very marginal victory over his enemy. He would have to war with the same enemy repeatedly. It did not have to be this way. God gave King Joash an opportunity to win a decisive victory, but Joash was too casual about it.

Unfinished victories, and incomplete battles, accumulate with new ones until we become overwhelmed. Win every war completely and even beyond what seems necessary at that time. Take personal initiative and push things beyond what is a minimal effort. We are far too casual with those things that seek to destroy us. We are not generous enough in our love and Christian responses toward the Lord. Compromise is very costly. Do not only cause the enemy to regress for a season and then return to defeat you. Pursue and complete the battle. Demoralize the devil in your life completely. Put some wide margins between the enemy and yourself by being deliberately aggressive in a good way.

There is a great story that further underscores this truth of healthy margins in our lives. The man's name is Caleb. He was Joshua's partner in vision and faith. When Israel ultimately came into the land of promise, there was still an unconquered region which giants occupied. Caleb was not happy with this constant looming threat to Israel's safety and peace. Caleb took passionate initiative even in his senior years and conquered the giants. He offered to do this. Caleb was not asked by Joshua to fight these threatening enemies. Caleb's passion for the promise motivated him to move beyond the basic and into abundance.

Do not wait till you first are attacked or confronted with resistance to your vision and dreams. Search out those things which could possibly compromise your success. Do not wait to be told to do it. Take initiative and create an opportunity for advancement, while creating as safe a distance as possible with that which would hinder. It's time to turn the tables and pursue the enemy rather than being pursued.

David's pebble stone was great to knock the enemy down. But David took the sword and removed Goliath's head permanently. This was initiative that completed the victory over the giant. He could never rise again and threaten God's people. Suppressing him was not enough.

Many times the enemy is pushed back only a little. Instead of defeating him completely, we only suppress him temporarily. The same is done with problems, habits, and spiritual battles. Our victories are too indecisive. We are more than conquerors. A greater space must be obtained between us and the enemy.

Jesus came to give us life and that more abundantly (John 10:10). The very nature of God is to do exceedingly abundantly above all we can even ask or imagine (Eph. 3:20). We are more than conquerors (Rom 8:37). This means we attain victories in Christ that are far beyond just barely making it. In Jesus, we do not just defeat the enemy. We defeat him beyond just moving him back a little. We put a major margin between victory and failure, poverty and prosperity. So many are just borderline Christians. When the slightest negative happens in their lives, they slip into defeat and failure. Such people have not taken extra initiative and created large margins between the enemy and themselves.

It means getting the enemy away from the borders of our lives. Too many live too close to the edge. One tiny slip and they go over the edge. The enemy waits and watches for someone to be inattentive just one time and easily fail because of not having enough space between victory and failure.

Many cross their Jordan, defeat a walled Jericho, and park there. Such victories are gateways to bigger ones waiting to be conquered. God's promise is far greater than hanging around the borders of His blessings. What we may consider to be the finish line, God sees as our starting line.

The promise land was occupied by other nations while God's people were in Egypt. These nations became Israel's enemies when Israel was moving into their promise. It became necessary to force these people out and possess what God had promised to them.

No blessing just sits waiting for us to possess it. It is usually possessed illegally by something or someone else. Any blessed place will be occupied by something else if we neglect to possess what is ours. Spiritual warfare is often required in areas of our lives, in order to receive and experience what is ours. Enemies, such as self-centeredness, greed, slothfulness, and passivity, could prevent us from receiving the blessings promised to us.

Whatever we deem the enemy of our success to be, it must be thoroughly dealt with. Certain issues in our lives cannot be temporarily suppressed only to raise their head at the wrong time in our progress to success. Generous margins must be created between what may hinder us and our goals.

Chapter Ten

Beyond Just Enough

TEN VIRGINS WERE invited to a notable wedding. They were responsible to lead the procession as the groom was ushered to meet his bride at the celebration. Lamps were required, since it could end up being at night. These lamps were to be full of oil, wicks trimmed and ready to be lit a moment's notice.

The bride groom did not arrive at the anticipated time. It became very late and all ten virgins fell asleep. All their lamps ran out of oil and died. All were invited to the celebration. All came to wait. They all brought their lamps. They were all virgins. All their lamps went out, and they all fell asleep. So many things were similar about the ten... except that five made it to the celebration, and five did not.

Not only were they gravely disappointed in missing the wedding celebration but they were very severely punished.

The groom expected a lot better from them. Because they were chosen to serve the entire party in a very special way, which required the lamps, the groom expected all of them to make sure they did not run out of oil. In this realm of honour, they did not need to be told to take extra oil. This is something people of leadership plan for.

None of the ten virgins intended to run out of oil. But, for some reason, none of them blew their lamps out to preserve the oil for a priority moment. Their weariness caught them by surprise. They were a whole lot more tired than they expected. Sometimes we wait too long to take a break in our lives of busyness. We do not realize how weary we are becoming. At some point, we will crash without warning and at the most awkward time in our life. A whole bunch of less significant activities can wear us out and we will miss the significant one.

Take short breaks in life, even if it is for a few hours. Perhaps you can only afford to take a day for a break to unwind from daily tension. Do not wait to take a vacation when you desperately need it. In that case, one cannot enjoy a vacation fully. Take a break or a vacation when you *don't* think you need it. When an important event comes, your lamp will shine brightly to fulfil and savour the moment.

What saved the five wise virgins from disqualification to the celebration was the extra oil they took with them. This was a very wise initiative on their part. It does not seem apparent that the five wise virgins were instructed to do this. It cost them extra money. It was inconvenient to carry the extra oil. However, that act is what qualified the five wise virgins to lead the procession and enter the wedding celebration.

Leaders pre-calculate all possible scenarios and prepare for them. Usually very little catches a good leader by surprise. They take action without being coerced to do so. No one has to tell them what to do. While others doze in comfort and convenience, leaders sacrifice. They predict the unpredictable and prepare. They are ready to wake up when an opportunity announces its arrival and embrace it.

Wise people always make an effort to create healthy margins in their lives. For them, just enough is not good enough. Christ himself said that He gives us life and that more abundantly. Life to spare and share because of healthy excess. This is where being more than conquerors comes into focus. Create a lot of space between failure and success. In all areas of life, do not depend on what is barely enough. Challenge yourself to go above and beyond. Beyond just obedience. Anticipate wisely what needs to be done and do it before you are told to. That's a leader.

So many Christians operate on just a bare minimal survival mode. Minimum church attendance, a bit of prayer, a pinch of praise, and touch of tithing. A short hurried devotional, a short scripture like "Jesus wept". But who will weep at midnight when your calculations are wrong and your lamp is out? You will. Who will be standing outside while kingdom celebrations are going on inside? It will be those who are not diligent enough to take that extra oil with them. Do more than marginally just enough.

A man came to Jesus and asked Him what he must do to have eternal life. Jesus told him to keep the commandments. The man's response was unique. He said, "Which ones?" Wow. In other words, he was saying, which ones can I keep and which ones can I neglect and still have eternal life. He wanted maximum blessings with minimum response. No abundant mentality here.

Chapter Eleven

Beyond the Common (part one)

THE BIBLE GIVES an account of a very notable woman from the city of Shunam. Her house was located along a very busy road that led in and out of the city. Daily, she positioned herself in her house so that she could observe the multitudes passing by. It is likely she looked out her kitchen window, which usually faced the road. From this position, she could observe the human traffic.

She was not just being unnecessarily nosey; she had a purpose for watching the crowds. Her reason for this was to spot the new successor of Elijah. Since she was a notable woman, she was very well aware concerning the affairs of the nation. Some believe this woman might have been involved in some way in the political aspect of the nation. For this reason, she might have known Elijah.

No doubt she heard that Elisha had received a double portion of God's power for his prophetic ministry. The news was out throughout the entire country that Elisha was now wearing Elijah's mantle. The manner by which Elijah departed added to the fascination of seeing Elisha. But more than that, she wanted to participate in this next glorious experience through Elisha.

It is interesting that a woman of notability was at home doing regular household duties. They had no children, her husband worked in their fields, and it does seem they had servants working for them. Perhaps this was just one of those times when you are in transition.

There are times in our lives when we find ourselves between experiences, levels, or seasons. It is when the former era fades and the new one has not yet fully arrived. The darkest hour of a day is midnight, right between the end of one day and the beginning of another. The former day ends with darkness and the new one begins with darkness. Between two high places, there is always a valley, and in some cases, a canyon. Transition is very challenging. Many fail in this season.

The prophet Habakkuk cried out to the Lord while he and the nation were in transition. He asked the Lord to revive them in the midst of the years. In other words, he asked the Lord to preserve and sustain him during the time in between. It's the time between the promise given and the promise fulfilled. Between deliverance and promise is the wilderness. It's the time between the starting line and finish line.

The idea of moving from glory to glory sounds wonderful, except for the time in between. Every process of advancement has a zero time when nothing seems to be happening. Have hope, a new day will come for sure. God will see to it, just be patient and wait on the Lord. A moment will come when you will know what initiative to take and introduce a new day. God will help you negotiate the time in between.

At such challenging times, it is possible to become impatient and make bad decisions—decisions that can greatly hamper reaching our destination. Abraham could not wait for his miracle. He took Hagar and had a baby with her. God did not accept Ishmael as the son of inheritance. Ultimately, Abraham's impatience created long lasting problems for many generations.

There are those who wait for something to happen so they can respond. These are wonderful people but have no realized leadership potential in them. Others who make it happen have realized the leader in them. These succeed in life beyond the level of existence. This woman was a leader. House duties did not prevent her from finding a window through which her next level of experience would come.

Moses became impatient in not seeing God's people delivered soon enough and killed a man. Abraham became anxious about the promise of God becoming fulfilled and produced

Ishmael. Peter got nervous for Jesus and cut a man's ear off. Jacob wanted the blessing immediately, that very night, before morning, and ended up limping the rest of his days. Many others did typical things trying to expedite the promise.

God did not approve any one of these actions but neither condemned those who took them. What these people did in their anxious moment was not ideal. However, God was pleased not with what they did but with the fact that they did *something*. In each of these cases, God still blessed these individuals because at least they had done something.

Initiatives are difficult. There is no manual on how to blaze a new trail. There is no instruction book on what to do perfectly right to get to the next level. Unless we are willing to put up with some mess, wrong turns, detours, and back tracking, we will never discover new territory. You would never have children if you thought birthing them and raising them was a squeaky clean process. View your mistakes, failures, wrong turns, and misses in the rear-view mirror. The windshield of your future is much larger.

Moses was wrong in the way he handled his call. However, he did something. The rest complained and murmured but did nothing about it. They just stayed in injustice and cruelty. No one dared think beyond the box of the bondage they were in. They had been so long in this state of slavery that they thought it was normal.

Peter could not wait for Jesus to come into the boat and still the storm. He had never walked on water before, but he would now, even in a storm. He began to sink halfway there. Jesus reached out and saved him. Others would rather stay in a storm-tossed boat, with the possibility of sinking, than walk to Jesus. The risk is the same but the reward is different. You can either take a risk and sink with the boat or take the risk and sink while walking to Jesus. I'll take Jesus!

Moses' mistake ran him into the burning bush. Esau ran Jacob into Bethel. Peter, though ambitious and tripping over his own feet, was the first one to preach the Pentecost message. Religion ran Jesus into the experience of the cross. He could not have had the experience of the power of His resurrection without it. Initiative costs but pays off.

The four walls of the Shunamite's home did not prevent her from expecting a new day in her life. She did not allow the common activities of the home to cloud new possibilities. She found a window of hope to look through. The window faced the traffic of possibility. The new prophet, with a double anointing, sooner or later would pass by. She made sure that she was not going to miss her opportunity passing by.

Every wall has a door and every mountain range has a passage. Every wilderness has a path and every fenced in experience has a gate. The Red Sea can part, the Jordan can roll back, and the wilderness can blossom as a rose. The sun and moon can stand still; God just needs someone to take initiative.

She looked for an opportunity to do something for someone else. One good way to deal with most depression in transition is to invest in someone else. As we will see in a few pages from now, she did what she could and heaven did what only heaven can do. It was when Joseph interpreted the dreams of others that his own dream was fulfilled. The fulfilment of your dream is when you assist in seeing the dreams of others come true.

Multitudes run from sea to sea, event to event, and seminar to seminar, looking for a new experience—a new day. I saw a funny cartoon showing four fences coming together at the intersection of four pastures. There were four cows each stretching their necks through the barb wire fence into the next cow's pasture. Each one was reaching for what appeared to be greener grass on the other side. Remember, the grass is just as green where you are, so enjoy it. Right where you are is the potential for all you need.

The supernatural is usually cloaked in the common. The divine came packaged in humanity and religion missed it. Jesus was born to two ordinary people in a barn, announced to plain shepherds and later followed by fishermen. He came within view of the synagogue, brushed by religion, but was not identified. He joined His voice with the rabbis, walked their roads, ate their food, and shopped in their markets.

Yet He was unknown, overlooked, and unnoticed as the Messiah—God with us in all His fullness.

This woman of Shunam was unique. From the place of the common and ordinary, she personally took initiative to seek a new day. Somehow she believed there was something extra ordinary in a regular crowd. Though every day seemed to be the same, she felt that there was a special one which would transform all that was common. She believed a greater future could begin right from where she was.

The day did come when she spotted the doubly anointed prophet of the Most High God. Indeed he was wearing the mantle she had previously seen on Elijah. Now the critical moment had come. What would she do? Was there action and initiative she could take to engage the opportunity? Opportunity is within reach... now what?

It is not enough to spot new opportunities. Jesus passed by many people with needs. Only those who cried out for mercy were blessed. One only wonders how many people Jesus passed by and their needs were not met. They did not press through the crowd, nor take the roof off. Perhaps they did nothing to position themselves where they could engage. The Bible says we should seek, ask, and knock, and such will be rewarded. Scripture says that all who call will be saved. Those who confess Jesus will experience transformation. God will never force you; you must take action, be aggressive, and dare to trust God. A turtle goes nowhere until it sticks its neck out.

Imagine stepping out of her house, breaking into the travelling crowd, and stopping the prophet to invite him in for lunch. What a challenging move. So many things could have held her back. "What if he thinks I'm weird?" "What will other people say when they see this?" "How will I feel if Elisha refuses to accept the invitation?" It is the negative "what ifs" that prevent us from taking a step of faith. People of initiative only possess positive "what ifs".

It's the negative ones that kill so many dreams and visions. Opportunities slip by our window because of the fear the negative "what ifs" produce. It paralyses initiative, which engages the supernatural and ushers in a new era. Why could we not convert the negative "what ifs" to positive, faith-sourced ones? *What if this is my moment, my day, and the key to my next level?*

Just think, this same man of God walked by numerous homes and kitchen windows. Many others had the same opportunity to experience the new anointing. But most were too occupied with regular life and its pressing concerns. They were totally unaware of the prophet passing by their dwelling. It was life as usual. But it was in the usual that the unusual was. That is the easiest place to miss the spectacular.

At her first invitation, Elisha *did* decline. She was not deterred. It just brought out her leadership determination.

The Bible says that she constrained him to come and have a meal. The word constraining is a very strong word. It means to get hold of what you envision, seizing it with courage. It implies that one cannot be casual about your pursuit. It also means to bind a decision upon yourself in such a determined manner that there is no possible way you could be personally separated from it by anything. It is a decisive initiative... so determined it is irreversible. Wow. She constrained Elisha to come in and have a meal. That's powerful.

Do not shrink back from your pursuit when resistance occurs. Pass the pride test of possible rejection. Jesus was severely resisted when He determined to accomplish salvation by the cross. He did not shrink back into self-pity and quit. Press for the mark of the high calling in Christ Jesus; don't just try for the "whatever". Everyone has a dream, but nothing happens until the dream has you.

This woman indeed was one who advanced in life, moving from one level of success to another. She was not motivated by desperation or needs. Those who are motivated to get help because they have needs stop moving forward when their needs are met. This woman was one who had a true spirit to advance, and "press for the mark of the high calling", as Apostle Paul said, not just the average.

Elisha did not appear to have any desperate needs. He did not look hungry. He was not going door to door begging for help. He was not sleeping under a bridge. This woman was not obligated nor motivated to do something for the prophet because of a need.

In the last few years, the world has experienced so many tragic events. Literal catastrophes have occurred over and over again, creating desperate needs right around the globe. Numerous governments, organizations, agencies, societies, and even financially blessed individuals have made noble attempts to help.

It became necessary to expose these needs to the world, appealing for assistance. More and more, technology is used to do this and that is a good thing. Graphic pictures of tragic conditions are repeatedly flashed on our screens daily, in hopes of a favourable response. While all this is necessary, it preconditions the viewing public to only respond to the desperate and urgent. The desperate and urgent has to be presented more and more effectively, since the viewing public becomes increasingly calloused.

Giving and helping because of desperate needs is definitely a great thing to do. But there is another level of giving. It is giving beyond being motivated by compassion. It is giving to bless, to prosper, and to support *preventative* initiatives not only corrective ones. This kind of giving reduces the need for giving into very urgent situations. A lot of helping and giving has been done this way recently.

The idea is to be self-motivated in giving, before the cries of the world become so desperate. In church, God did not say to tithe and give offerings by being obligated with the church's financial need. Most of the church's financial problems are due to the lack of giving as simple obedience from a heart of love. Giving motivated by desperate financial needs usually only lasts until there is no need. Once people have learned to give because of being need-motivated, the danger is that a need has to be created to perpetuate continual giving.

The Shunamite woman took initiative and chose to bless Elisha without him being in a desperate need. When is the last time you blessed someone who did not need a blessing? We are too need-motivated and not enough faith and blessing-motivated in our giving.

Abraham was a blessed man when God instructed us to bless him (Gen 12:1-3). Abraham was to bless all the nations of the world. He was not mandated to respond to their crises. In other words, Abraham was called to bless the world. God prospered a prosperous man so that He could communicate the same to millions.

Giving to needs is the level of giving which most people practise. If the same poor require continued help, then we are not giving them the help they really need. They must learn how to sacrifice and save seed to produce a harvest—a multiplied return. Poverty is not only physical lack but wrong thinking. The Bible says that as a man thinks in his heart so is he. Out of the heart come the issues of life. Prosperity begins in our thinking, not in our pockets.

When giving to the blessed, the blessed are blessed because they sow, invest, and multiply what they receive. What we give the blessed will be multiplied through them. So many wait for the blessed to give to them. When what is given is consumed instead of sown, one remains in lack and poverty. What we sow, we reap. That truth is for the rich *and* for the poor who need plenty.

Scripture says God gives bread to the eater but seed to the sower. God does not have to give bread to the sower, because he produces his own bread in harvest. Always sow in good soil for a great harvest.

The apostle Paul in Philippians 4:19 said that God will supply all our needs according to his riches in glory. Notice that God will not supply according to our needs but "according to his riches in glory". That's rich. That kind of supply totally obliterates every need in existence. Giving to bless is giving beyond the demand or a command. It is not limited to obedience but to generosity. In fact, you do not have to wait for God to tell you what to do or how much to give. That is what a servant would do. A King does not wait to be told; he makes a decision and does it.

Scripture says in Ephesians 3:20 how God will do exceedingly abundantly above all that we ask or think, according to the power that works in us.

John 10:10 says that Jesus does not only give us life but abundant life. In the beatitudes, Jesus said that when you give you receive so much that it is pressed down, shaken together, and still running over. God gives to bless. God does not limit His giving to us by our needs. He gives because He indeed is the King of kings and Lord of lords.

The woman, while looking for Elisha to pass by, took initiative to be prepared the day she saw him. Every day the house was ready to host the prophet. An extra table setting, a place to sit, more food in the oven, and more fresh bread. It is possible she chose not to host a lot of people for that season, since she did not know when Elisha would come by. Her house was ready.

There are times when we need to limit multiple activities in our lives while we wait for the Lord. You cannot be so busy and still host God's presence in your life. Life is so demanding that it can choke out the more important things. We make appointments for so many things in our lives, and yet when it comes to the Lord, it seems He has to just fit into *our* schedule.

This woman did not wait to be told what to do. No one told her to have her house ready for the prophet. She made that decision. This is a leadership-minded individual. These are the characteristics of a leader. No excuses, no procrastination, just aggressive and calculated initiatives.

Elisha came by her house numerous times. She studied his times and movements. It may have appeared to others as unpredictable but not to this woman. She studied the movements of the prophet, becoming acquainted with the movements of the supernatural. That is how she knew when to be out on the road and intercept the prophet. The Holy Spirit is not unpredictable except to our own set timings. All God does has a divine pattern. When we take time and interest, we will learn the ways and manners of the Holy Spirit and respond accordingly. This way we are not waiting at the bus depot when God is at the airport.

Progressive people do not stop being ambitious. The woman hosted Elisha every time he came by. What a wonderful experience that must have been for the house. Elisha probably shared the miraculous things God was doing in the land. How exciting and interesting. However, this woman did not stop at this point. She had more vision in mind.

The brief visitations of the prophet were not enough for this aggressive woman. Many would have been happy to settle with visitations. She wanted to have a place for the prophet to dwell, not just visit. This required further action and sacrifice.

She talked to her husband about expanding their house to accommodate the prophet and the prophetic permanently. Their dwelling had to be redesigned, furniture rearranged, finance expanded. The movement of the Holy Spirit will always cause readjustments in our lives. He will first visit as is, but in order to inhabit, dwell, and live where we live, restructure is necessary.

Jesus said that the birds of the air have nests and foxes have holes, but the son of man has nowhere to lay His head. Jesus was not referring here to a physical place. He had a place of abode. It is in the same context as when He said, 'Destroy this building (referring to the temple), and in three days I will raise it up.'

The issue here was that Jesus did not have a place at that time where He could exercise His headship on the earth. For this reason, Jesus said, "I will build my church and the gates of hell will not prevail." So Jesus is the head of the body called the Church. That is how and where He is exercising His will and purpose on the earth.

The New Covenant experience provides a dwelling place for God. This is what separates Christianity from all other religions. Many have some type of supernatural visitations, even from God. The Holy Spirit visits many and draws them toward a new Covenant experience. Only the born-again experience gives God a place to dwell. That is the most profound and miraculous experience a human being could ever have. Just to think that the Almighty has chosen to dwell in us as His temple!

One particular day, the prophet and his servant requested an audience with the woman. Elisha asked her how he could bless her for all she had done for them. She did not request anything from the prophet for a reward. This was not her motive. She did it solely because that was what was in her heart. A reward is always certain, because God is faithful, but she did not expect it.

Elisha decreed that she would have a baby boy. It did not matter to the Word of the Lord that she was barren and her husband was old. God's word and its fulfilment is not based on our conditions. God's word comes from heaven's throne and does not need earth's help. In the very room she provided for the prophetic is where she was blessed with a miracle.

The husband was busy with the harvest in the field. There is no indication that he was in the prophet's room with his wife when she got the prophet's word. There is something powerful we must notice here. The husband received a miracle also, even though he was not present at the moment of the word of healing.

The blessings of the Lord are transferred to all who are in covenant with the one blessed. The husband of this woman was blessed in his old age with the ability to cause conception. He was not physically present with his wife when she received the word of prophesy. But, since they were in covenant, he got blessed while still working in the field.

Abraham's great-great grandson Levi was accredited by Abraham's tithing. Generations which were not born yet were in line for a blessing because of their forefather's giving. Covenants are God's divine network by which He blesses the generations to come. God's favour flows through righteous lineages. God told Abraham He would bless him and his seed.

When we entered into a blood-related covenant with Jesus, we were aligned to receive all He was blessed with. Jesus put us in line with all of heaven's blessing. Not only us but all those who are in covenant relationship with us. Parents, you have the total biblical support by which to transfer the blessings of the Lord from your lives to your offspring. Even in relationships that are not naturally blood related, but embrace a spiritual father and mother, such people receive their blessings.

God ordained ministry to bless His people. In Numbers 6:22-27, the Lord instructed Moses and Aaron on how to bless Israel. They were to also invoke the name of the Lord upon them. Abraham was called to bless all the families of the world through his seed (Gen 12:1-3). Jesus was that seed (Gal 3:16). Church members would do well for themselves to walk in a covenant relationship with the ministry God ordained. Respect and honour would be the channels through which the blessings would be transmitted.

If you want to have friends and family who can bless you, bless. Reduce or eliminate enemies by love. Love flows to a thousand generations. All those down-line from you—associated with you—are positioned for the blessing of the Lord through you. That is why the enemy attacks relationships, so he can cut off the flow of blessing. That is why Malachi 4:5-6 calls for natural and spiritual families to be restored to biblical relationship. Satan's attack, especially on fatherhood in our day, is a clear indication that he wants to curb lineage blessings.

Chapter Twelve

Beyond the Common (part two)

A BOY WAS BORN to the Shunamite couple, and before long grew up to be a fine young man. He was now old enough to assist his father in the field of harvest. All seemed so well until one alarming day, when the boy experienced a severe pain in his head, which totally immobilized him. A young lad working with him in the field carried him home to his mother. He died on his mother's knees, while she tried to comfort him.

I want to take this account and metaphorically extract certain truths, which are eternal. Such truths can be applicable to any age. Times and situations may come and go but truth does not age or change. Truth is sourced in the Holy Spirit and therefore inherently contains eternal qualities (2 Tim. 3:16). It is profitable in every era.

First of all, we want to quickly reflect on this woman, who was barren. Spiritually speaking, God has numerous times in the Bible given miracle sons to barren women. The Church may have experienced some barrenness in the last season. Certain statistics seem to claim that numerically we have not reproduced well. This may be a concern to us, and to some degree, rightfully so. However, we (like this woman) are taking initiative and hosting the prophetic in our churches. We are making room for the prophetic to have a permanent place of function in our churches. Prophetic visitations are also well embraced. This can mean only one thing: A new miraculous generation is being conceived and born. This generation, like the young boy, will not be the product of human nor religious efforts. It will be the result of the word of the Lord declared by the spirit of the prophetic by all sectors of our church ministries.

Secondly, this miraculous generation will mightily assist to bring in our Father's harvest. The former generation pioneered, cleared land, ploughed, and sowed for years. Much sacrificially. Now the harvest is ready to be brought in. These will be the young men and women who will do it under the mature supervision of the patriarchs.

Thirdly, what about the pain in the head of this young lad? It was Satan's attempt to immobilize this generation from doing God's kingdom work. Humanistic philosophies, anti-God teachings, literally doctrines of devils have permeated our learning centres from pre-school to the top learning centres of our day. That is the pain in the head—in the thinking of our young generation—which is inflicted by Satan. What is so sad and disturbing is that it is not the young generation engineering this curse. It is the past generation devoid of the mind of Christ, barren in their thinking, and not having the mind of Christ.

Much of today's secularized education excludes Jesus Christ. He is the source of all knowledge and wisdom. Adam and Eve, in the garden, pursued the tree of knowledge, leaving out the wisdom with which knowledge safely operates. It became a destructive move on their part, just like today's penchant for gathering knowledge, at the exclusion of God's wisdom, has become.

The Bible is not allowed as a text book, or even a devotional, in our so-called learning centres. We are actually foolish enough to think we can write a better one. The very life of the Holy Spirit is ignored and avoided. Prayer, if any, is so generic that it is powerless to have any effect or transformation of the human heart and mind. These compromises have resulted in our classrooms becoming terrorized by radicals making these once-secure places unsafe.

Christ-less education has deprived society of the wisdom it so desperately needs to be successful. Rational thinking sourced in the mind of Christ has been lost. Bazaar and radically extreme behaviour is out of control. This is the pain in the head that is immobilizing our communities from functioning the way God originally intended. Like the Shunamite's son, too many are taken out of being a positive contribution to our Father's kingdom.

A young man, who worked in the field with this lad, carried him to his mother. This is a great picture of the young generation appealing to the former generation for help. A generation helping one another, knowing where to go for help. It is very probable that this young man heard about the boy's mother relating to the prophetic—perhaps also knowing that the young man now ill was a miracle child. The generation God is raising up is appealing to the supernatural. They have realized that when a crisis comes, philosophy and theory is not enough. The power of God in the miraculous is needed.

This is the woman who intercepted the prophet and brought the power of the prophetic into her house. She fed the prophet, gave him space in the house, embracing his supernatural dimension. When the prophet's word came to her, she believed it and a miracle happened.

The miracle God originally gave this woman expired right on her knees. This was not acceptable to this woman of courage. What would have been the end for some was just the beginning of another miracle for her. What she did with her son is an incredible story.

She did not call the funeral home to pick up her son. No. She was not going to let anyone embalm her miracle. She hosted Elisha long enough to know that when one level of blessing is finished and taken away, it makes room for a greater one. She understood that a Hebrew day started with night and broke into the brilliance of morning after the darkest time.

The Shunamite mother took the lifeless boy into the prophet's chamber. This is the place she prepared for the supernatural in her home and family. Certainly the son must have helped his mother to maintain this room for Elisha's comfort. He was there many times before on his own, but now was carried in. It is good to be acquainted with the divine dimension long before you need it.

Bringing the lifeless body of her son into the prophet's chamber positioned him for a supernatural experience. The initiative she took to build this room for the prophet now was serving her as a blessing. When she built this prophet's chamber, she was meeting someone else's need, not her own. Now the blessing was returning to her. The former generation must do everything they can to make room for the supernatural and position the new generation within it.

Have you received something from God in a miraculous way but without warning, in the midst of working in the harvest, it expired? You held it tightly in your arms, you prayed and cried, but to no avail. It died. It could be a dream you had for yourself or even your children. Maybe your ministry, your calling, or business. You had hope and vision but something happened and it was marred and shattered. Perhaps it's your faith, your walk with God, which has slowly diminished. Unfulfilled prophecies, promises you have not reached. Be encouraged, you have done nothing wrong. This woman did nothing wrong and lost her miracle. But even if we failed, made a mistake, or did the wrong thing, we have forgiveness from God. It is complete, totally restorative, and not punishing since Christ took all of our punishment. Do not blame yourself or others for your miracles fading away. All that will do is embalm your miracle. Yes, there is something you can do in the midst of discouragement, despair, and dismay.

Some read history, others make it. Some wait for the right atmosphere, others create it. Some love to see miracles, while others produce them. Some talk faith, others live it. This is who this woman was. She made history, created the atmosphere of faith, experienced one miracle, and did something to position herself for the next one.

When things are down and out, you cannot revive yourself; you cannot restore life nor lift your faith back to its glory by yourself. If you could you wouldn't be where you are at in discouragement, having secretly quit on the inside. At this point, many well-meaning Christians say ridiculous and even irritating things. Things like, "Just believe." Thanks. How do I believe when my faith is in the ditch?

All you can do at this point, and all you need to do, is just position yourself in the presence of God. Do not try so hard to do something you cannot. Do not try and feel His presence; when the Holy Spirit blesses you, and He will, you will know it. The chaos was simply positioned where the Spirit of the Lord moved and His word was spoken. The chaos got a new day; it became the garden it never was and so will you. The dry bones of the valley could not do a thing to become a great army. They could not even live on their own, let alone become a mighty army. They too were laid out and positioned before the Word of the Lord. They did nothing except lay there in God's presence. His presence did it all. Relax, quit striving, just position yourself in the Almighty presence of God and enjoy the ride.

This is exactly the initiative this woman took. All she could do was position her dead miracle where God would eventually move through His prophet. She could not revive him, but she knew God could.

The husband questioned his wife why it was necessary and seemingly so urgent to find the man of God. She did not tell him their son was dead. Nor did she tell the husband why she needed the prophet to come immediately. All she said was "All is well". Her son was dead, her miracle had expired, and this woman said, "All is well."

It is not wise to expose your faith ventures while they are still in their infancy stage. Not everyone has the same level of faith. The one God gives a challenge is also the one God supplies the kind of faith to perform it. It is unfair to expect others to fully feel the same way we do about faith ventures that God gives to us personally. Be cautious to whom you expose the delicate things God gives you to experience and believe. Unnecessary exposure to where we are at, and to what we are doing about it, exposes us to too much advice from well-meaning people. There are things that must be kept between you and your God alone.

In another miracle, in another time, Jesus removed all the mourners from the house before He raised a young girl from the dead. They were not bad people, but they had a very low ceiling of faith in Jesus and His ability. Their unbelief could prevent what God wants to do, especially in the early stages of a vision. Give your faith venture, your fresh vision, time to mature before you allow everybody to have an opinion on it. Be like Mary, the mother of Jesus, and run to someone like Elizabeth who also was experiencing a new faith venture. Stay there for a while and let faith develop the vision before others get involved. Choose your faith partners well.

She took her servant and told him to ignore her comfort and get to the prophet as quickly as possible. What a woman of initiative! She did not wait to be told what to do. She did not look for pity nor stand around blaming others for her situation. None of this would bring life and resurrection to what had died. In fact being bitter or even angry with the lord would be like wrapping your expired miracle up in grave clothes. She had one sure hope, and that was to bring God onto the scene of this darkness. And that's what she did.

Consider this woman's confession of faith. Her miracle son is dead and she tells her questioning husband that all is well. When the prophet enquires of her what the urgency is all about, she says that all is well. Remember that her miracle child is dead while her confession is alive. Your condition will adjust to your confession. Do not adjust your language to your situation. You speak the language of heaven, if heaven is what you want. Let earth adjust to heaven, death to life, and defeat to victory, by the words you choose to speak. It's your call!

What she saw in the supernatural realm was summoned into the physical realm by her confession of true faith. Her confession described what faith saw and not what her physical eyes saw. She saw what was already accomplished in the invisible sphere and brought it into the natural, revolutionizing it. This was not based on human feelings or evaluation of the natural. She deliberately chose to exercise her faith and speak accordingly. She had to speak beyond her feelings of shock, sorrow, despair, and pain. She could not obey these feelings and affirm them with her words.

Do not stay speechless when the enemy blasts you with negative words and experiences. Use the Word as the Sword of the Spirit and pierce the power of Satan's assault. He is a liar. Contradict everything he says and every thought he gives. When he says that it's the end, tell him that every end has a new beginning. Every midnight is an announcement that morning has just arrived. Morning is not when the sun begins to shine; morning is one second after midnight. It still may be very dark. There may not be a ray of morning light yet. But regardless of how dark it is, morning will certainly come. Don't sleep through it; be ready for it.

It is very important to stay in touch with what God is doing and saying today. The Spirit of God is moving mightily in the world. Be aware of what ministries God has provided locally and globally. When this woman's crisis came, she knew where to go. She knew where the man of God was. Staying up to date with the supernatural movements of the Holy Spirit will be advantageous in time of need or advancements to a new level. Her initiative to host the prophetic was now paying off. She did not have to try and figure out where to find what she needed. Relate to the movements of the Holy Spirit long before you need to engage them.

Invest time, energy, and money into good ministries. Sow into them like the woman did into Elisha. But don't sow only when you need a harvest immediately. Support and sow into such ministries long before you even know you will have a need. Do not treat God or His ministries like a gambling slot machine, where you put a few dollars in hoping to get back a lot. Treat God's kingdom like a field. Sow and harvest!

Elisha suggested Gehazi go in his stead, but the woman held on to Elisha's feet until he consented to go himself. If anyone could understand this determination, he could. This is how he unwaveringly pursued his spiritual father, Elijah, for the double portion. God is never upset with us when we refuse second best and demand the best. God cannot answer second-best prayers, because heaven does not have second-best answers. Upgrade your prayers to match heaven's best.

In 2 Kings 4:30, the Bible says Elisha arose and followed the woman back to her house, to the prophet's chamber. This is a very interesting picture. Elisha knew where this woman's house was. Why did he need to follow her? One would think she should now follow the man of God and not the other way around!

To answer this, we refer to Rev 3:20, where Jesus stands at the door and knocks. He does not just enter in. God gave us a realm of responsibility and authority. He will not arbitrarily enter in until we open the door and invite Him. He wants to partner together. God will not impose Himself upon us and violate our will. However, He will answer when we call, He will respond when we confess, and He will be found when we seek.

Would the blind men have been healed if they did not cry out, 'Lord, have mercy on us"? Would the ten lepers have experienced their miracle if they'd just remained quiet? What about the woman with the issue of blood, who pressed through the crowd? She touched the hem of His garment and was healed. What if she had said, "the Lord knows my need and my address"? She would not have tapped into the supernatural. The supernatural followed each of these people's effort and blessed them. Water follows the path you make for it; light shines where you give it passage.

The Bible says Elisha entered the room where the dead boy lay. Those who carry the supernatural are not afraid of places where the power of God is needed. There are those who claim to be so spiritual but only perform well where there is life. They criticize a dead church meeting but do not seem able to contribute life to it. If where you are is dead, bring life to it—communicate God's power. But don't be weird seeking attention, just be a life-line of blessing.

Elisha went into his prophet's room where the boy was. He closed the door and prayed. He also did something very unique. He placed his body on the boy's dead body. Head to head, eye to eye, mouth to mouth, hands to hands, and I suppose feet to feet. It seems like a strange manner by which to minister to a person. So why did Elisha do it this way?

Elisha acted out prophetically what God is saying to every generation. The ministries of God and the former generation must learn to relate to the next generation. If we cannot relate, we cannot communicate. We have anointing they need. We carry the life they need to function effectively in the kingdom of God. Technology has its place but cannot, and never will, replace personal relationships. Jesus did not send a photograph of Himself from heaven; He actually came in the flesh to accomplish the glorious salvation by grace.

Elisha placed himself on the dead body in order to bring resurrection life to it. Face to face for fellowship, eye to eye for vision communication. Mouth to mouth for speaking the language of heaven. Head to head for a new mind, heart to heart for new life. Knees to knees for humility and prayer. Feet to feet for a new walk with God. Hands to hands to do greater works of God than ever before.

The boy sneezed seven times and opened his eyes. What are those sneezes? This generation needs to be allowed to sneeze and get rid of impurities. They have been infected with ungodly philosophies by the former generation's backsliding education. As this generation experiences the entry of the supernatural, they will sneeze up a lot of dead garbage, even religious stuff.

Not everything the new generation does is perfect. As they move aggressively into new territory, it will not always be just divine action but also reaction. Every generation has experienced that. The former generation must reduce its criticism of the new, since that is who they raised in their own homes. If we do not totally like the product, check the source. Let's bless, be available, and bring resurrection life. After a few sneezes, the new generation will be ready to go back into the harvest.

This generation has made mistakes. They have failed, adopting new fads, even strange ones from around the world. Unique style, methods... the list goes on. We must hold this generation close to us and let them sneeze. The glory of God is resurrecting them to supernatural life and some of *us* from our traditional graveyards. If you pray for rain, be ready to put up with the mud puddles.

The bottom line is this: None of this could ever have happened unless someone like this Shunamite woman took the initiative she did. A simple lunch to host a prophet is where it all started. It ended as a powerful miracle, which served to birth new and greater beginnings.

Chapter Thirteen

Beyond Hospitality

O N THE ROAD from Jerusalem, two discouraged disciples of Jesus were walking home. Their hopes of Jesus being the king and overpowering the Roman rule had been shattered by the crucifixion. Confusion was added to discouragement when rumour was told about Jesus' possible resurrection.

It was evening and time to go home, have a good sleep, and see what the next day would bring. On their way home, they could not help but try to make sense of the barrage of activities. They did not have even the slightest clue of what they would experience in the next hours.

Is it not amazing that, as spiritual as we feel we might be, and for as long as we have walked with Jesus, we also don't always have a clue what God is about to do in our lives? Someone reading this may be at the same point in their typical condition as these two disciples were. Basically, they had just given up on it all. But someone special was about to catch up to them... and maybe to you.

They didn't know it yet, but in one hour, they would be running back to Jerusalem on this same road. In one hour, they would have a message that would revolutionize them and their brethren. In one hour, confusion and despair, hopelessness and dismay, would flee and disappear.

Jesus caught up to them, joining them on their walk. He unravelled scriptures for them so profoundly that it burned like Holy Fire deep in their souls. So far as they knew, He was only a common stranger travelling a typical, common road.

Just how possible was it that the King of Glory, the resurrected Christ, Jesus as God in the flesh was walking right next to them, and they did not see it? Just because we do not see Him does not mean He is not there. Just because we are so intoxicated with our opinions—our interpretations of events—we become blinded to the supernatural right beside us.

They finally arrived at the entrance to their home. The story could have ended there if they would not have taken initiative and been hospitable. This would determine the rest of the story.

What saved their day? It was the action they took in inviting Jesus to their house for a meal and to stay the night. Jesus did not ask them for it. When Jesus declined their first request, they constrained him to come in. It seems God tests the sincerity of our invitations.

At this time of the night, they could have found many valid reasons as to why they should not host this stranger. It was late, the children were in bed, the wife was not forewarned, and beds would have to be made. The whole house would be disturbed for one stranger. Taking initiative is never convenient. Usually, such opportunities show up at the most awkward time, and don't look significant enough to merit response. Jesus looked like just an ordinary stranger travelling somewhere. No fanfare, no chariots with white horses, just a stranger walking into the night without a halo.

Can you imagine preparing a meal for God? Had they known it was Jesus, the fullness of God, they would have said to the wife, "We just invited God for a meal!" Oh wow, talk about a nerve wracking experience. But as far as they knew, this was just a common stranger.

Here is something beyond interesting. They washed his feet and dried them with a towel. Did they not notice the nail scars? When they wiped His brow from the sweat of the journey and the dust of the day, did they not see His brow scored by the crown of thorns He had worn? When He took the bread in His hands to bless and break it, how could they miss the nail scars?

Just a short while before, a woman had broken the seal of an alabaster box and poured the expensive perfume on Jesus.

I believe the aroma stayed on Jesus through Gethsemane's agony, the judgement hall, the cross, the tomb, and the resurrection. Could they not smell the perfume that had filled the room when she poured it on Jesus? Could they not identify the same aroma coming from Jesus that night in their own house?

Jesus said that He would never leave us or forsake us. But in difficult times, have we not asked, 'Where is God?' He is there, but the natural blinds us to His presence. The common obscures the very son of God. He is there, with you; He cannot lie. Just because we do not recognize Him on our difficult journey, that does not mean He is not walking with us. His appearance may not be what we have expected, but look closely, and listen carefully. It's Him.

After all, did Jesus not tell them all this would happen? Oh yes, and what about His voice? They missed that also. Somehow their unbelief blinded them. It is really unbelievable that the Almighty Lord of Glory could be right so close and be undetected.

Many come to church and leave saying, "I didn't get anything out of the service." They might say the worship was not all that good. Perhaps they did not like something that did not fit their interpretation of how it should be. Yet, God was there in all His wonder and fullness. Yes, you can be where He is, and He can be where you are without you realizing it. Make sure you are aggressive enough to invite Him in.

As Jesus blessed the bread at the table, He opened their eyes and they saw Him. All of a sudden everything made sense. Then Jesus disappeared to go gather the rest of His scattered team. They too rushed back to Jerusalem to tell their comrades that Jesus was alive. When they got there, they did not have to tell the whole story, nor try to convince the rest, because Jesus had appeared to all of them.

It is amazing what blessings wait for us when we exercise self-motivation and do something we were not commanded to do. They invited Jesus to their house. They washed His feet without being asked. A meal was prepared, a place given to rest. All this without being told, begged, or obligated. That is where and when God will show up in a greater way. Step into a new mode of function. Do not wait to be asked, told, or commanded before you act.

The vast wilderness hosted a spectacular skyline. There was a unique pillar of fire and a cloud unmatched by any other. This was the scenery as God's people journeyed toward the Promised Land. No other wilderness could boast what this one was hosting.

Moses' tabernacle was in the midst of God's people, emanating the blessings and the glory of God over His people. This brought deliverance from slavery—not only healing but health to all the people. There was not one feeble one among them. They drank water out of the rock, ate heavenly food, and their shoes and apparel did not wear out. The cloud shaded them by day and the fire warmed them by night. They lived in Egypt in poverty but left in prosperity.

They saw Pharaoh severely dealt with, the Red Sea parting, and Pharaoh destroyed with his army. Eventually Jordan rolled back for them and Jericho's walls crumbled. Giants fell in defeat, larger armies than theirs ran for cover. God was in their midst and that is all that mattered. God's tabernacle was with them. No one could even imagine there could be more. Who would dare classify this experience as only a type and shadow of the reality still coming? But there was more.

We could become so intoxicated with a present level of God's glory that we become oblivious to the possibilities of anything greater. Israel embraced the types and shadows and made them their ideal. They parked, happy to remain at what was only a start—a beginning. They could not believe that there could be a greater and better covenant. The types and shadows became their ceiling. They fought for the former, defended it, and persecuted those who took initiative to move beyond that level. In it all, they missed the Messiah they had all been waiting for.

Like most of Israel, who stopped with Moses' covenant, we as Christians have built permanent belief structures around temporary revivals. Every move of God *contributes* to a greater ideal but in itself is *not* the ideal. Every phase of God's working in our lives must be adequately embraced but not stopped at.

Year after year Moses' tabernacle, its form of worship, and its function was maintained by the ordained priesthood. Though God ordained the priesthood to function at this level, it did not mean that they did not have an opportunity to go beyond it. All this was intended as an introductory level. God's glory was a lot more glorious than this, and God desired His people to experience it. But who would dare take it to another level. Who could believe that, for more, God needed someone who would respect the past but not be limited by it.

The Lord spotted just such a young man. He was out in the sheep pasture with his father's sheep. His name was David, the youngest of eight sons of Jesse. There was something about David that caught God's attention. There was a certain characteristic in David that God knew He could use to break the stagnant mold of the past and embrace a new and living way.

David was a man of personal healthy ambition. He did not wait around to be told what to do; he saw what needed to be done and did it. When the bear and the lion attacked his father's sheep, David did not only scare them away, he killed them. David was an enemy eliminator, not just a negotiator with an enemy of destruction. When David's father sent David to check on his brothers, David did not only temporarily knock out Goliath, but permanently took his head off of his body. David did not stand around getting advice from the fearful and unbelieving, he did something about it.

Moses' tabernacle's every aspect operated by command and precise order. It experienced a certain level of God's glory, which was very dynamic. It took millions of people through the wilderness, providing everything they needed to get to the ideal. Nations feared this presence of God in the midst of God's people. The effective function of this level, which was by command and obedience, determined Israel's victories.

Under various kings, who did not serve the Lord fully, the Ark of the Covenant was taken by the enemy for a short season. When it was retrieved, it was not put back into Moses' tabernacle. The Ark was placed in Kirjath-Jearim. It stayed there until King David made a place for it and brought it back to Israel. David did not take the Ark of the Covenant back to Moses' tabernacle.

David moved into a new day. He sailed through uncharted waters into a new era. He exemplified a new covenant relationship with God in Old Covenant times. David spiritually pioneered where there were no trails or maps to go by. David was not a map reader but a map maker. He did not look for worn-out old trails; he cut new ones. That's initiative beyond obedience to a command.

While many pined away at the degenerating power of the glory of God in their midst, David did something about it. He did not sit and discuss the negatives of the past nor glory in nostalgic memories. He got busy and built a new tabernacle for a new day. In the atmosphere of faith and love for God, he carved out a new day right in the presence of the old. It can be and must be done again, today.

Saul failed in his kingship. Samuel the prophet could not get over the fact that what he had anointed for a certain day was finished. It does not always mean it was wrong, just finished. That is difficult to comprehend. Moses' day was coming to a close. Saul's day of reigning shifted to David. Of course, that is challenging to humans, who find comfort in that which is predictable. But though predictable, God's spirit moves forward and we must too.

Excessive lengthy mourning about the end of the past demobilizes us from moving forward. At times it is our pride. We believe, like Samuel, that we did the right thing in the past. Samuel anointed Saul, and now it was over, making Samuel look mistaken in anointing Saul. God allows certain things from our past to diminish so that we are alerted to a greater future.

Samuels' unnecessary mourning for Saul caused him to overlook the emptiness of his horn of oil. Samuel was not ready to embrace a new day, because he could not let go of the former. It dried him out. God told the prophet first to quit mourning for the past. Secondly, to fill the horn with anointing oil. Thirdly, to rise up and anoint a new king. Do not die mourning for something God is done with.

The place David built for God's glory was noisy, loud, and alive with exuberant praise. There were instruments of music, choir arrangements, songs, and dance. The Glory of God was in view of the people and not hidden away. God affirmed David's initiatives by making Himself present among His people. Israel experienced great victories over their enemies. Initiative always moves forward, not backwards. Initiative does not repeat the past; it discovers a dynamic future, ready to possess greater promises. The good of the past becomes its seed of a greater future.

David respected the past but refused to be imprisoned or limited by it. He did not ignore the accomplishments of his forefathers. He used these accomplishments as a stepping stone for his new future. Dreams are not about yesterday but about a new day. Taking aggressive, unsolicited action to move forward is usually untraditional and unscripted. There are no manuals to go by. Manuals are written to describe what God has already done, not what He is going to do. Initiative is daring and unpredictable, requiring faith and exploits. The results are immeasurably rewarding.

Is it any wonder Jesus was called the son of David? Jesus came from the seed of David, and was called the root and offspring of David. The outpouring of the Holy Spirit was referred to as the restoration of David's tabernacle. Christ was raised to sit on David's throne. All this speaks very clearly that God operates through people who are willing to take a kind of new initiative into a new level in the Lord.

David's initiative made him a trailblazer. He even looked beyond his own day, preparing and planning for a temple beyond the one he built. He saw God's glory in greater ways for the future generations. A man of initiative does not get stuck with the past nor limited by the present. He does not park in his successes. He transfers them to a greater day for the next generation of God's people to move in.

When David's son Solomon became Israel's king, he moved with the same aggression. Solomon's temple exceeded in size and glory any structure of the past. He sacrificed beyond what was required by the former tabernacle. His generosity toward the Lord could not even be measured. He did all this without being commanded or demanded.

David became a New Testament man in Old Testament times. Solomon was given the privilege by the Lord to ask anything he desired and God would grant it. There was no greater king in Israel than David and no king more prosperous than Solomon. The rewards are unlimited for men and women who get a revelation of the unlimited God.

Chapter Fourteen

Beyond Generosity

CHRISTIANITY IS FAITH based. Those who try to understand before responding, compromise obedience. When obedience is compromised, so is its blessing. Teach in Biblical and necessary truths. God called teachers to unravel wonderful truths of God's word. Regardless of how well our minds are informed about sacred ways, our response to them must be by faith and not by human reasoning.

This same concept of faith response must be applied to tithing. The Lord has provided tremendous teaching concerning the tithe. Along with good teaching, there is also a lot of controversy about whether or not tithing is a new Covenant truth. Some believe it is, other believe it is not.

The intention of this chapter is not to adjust nor affirm either of these views on tithing. While the majority of the teaching is dynamic, our response to tithing must be simplified to an act of obedience by faith. Jesus said the kingdom of God is made up of little children. That being the case, a child's mind cannot even comprehend deep teaching on tithing. Yet a child will gladly and quickly respond to simple obedience to God's command.

Tithing was designed by God to be responded to by faith obedience. It is not to be understood but simply responded to. This response transcends all views, debates, and disagreements concerning the tithe. Faith does not require understanding for it to act. Nor does tithing require being understood for it to be a blessing. The tithe was to be obeyed, not understood.

Tithing by faith response is eating from the tree of life. Trying to understand it is eating from the tree of knowledge of good and evil. A faith response to tithing is trusting that God does know what is best for us, without having to figure it out. Trying to understand how certain sacred things work is like dissecting a frog in a lab; when you are done dissecting, it expires.

Making tithing appealing, by emphasizing its benefits, is circumventing a faith response. The truth of tithing does not need to be sold, just told, believed and responded to. Obedience is always blessed by God.

God asked Israel to bring numerous specified things to be sacrificed unto the Lord. Many of these sacrifices were put on an altar and burned. Certainly it seemed such a senseless thing to do. However, it was to be an act of faith obedience, even when it did not make sense to the human mind. If we challenge it, we are placing ourselves equal with God and His level of understanding. If a requirement is reasonable to the human mind before it is responded to, then faith and its blessing is annulled.

The tithe is a command of the Lord to be obeyed. This is the level of a servant's response. Many have stopped there. There is however a higher level of giving, which is the offering. The offering is not a commanded amount but rather what one offers from the heart. It is not manipulated or forced. No one has to tell one to do it. It is solely a decision one makes. It goes beyond obedience to a command.

If we have to be told what to do, it means we are still in a servant's status. We have not advanced to the next level, which is kingship. Until we handle commands properly in the servant status, graduation to rulership will not happen. The season of obedience is for the purpose of learning the heart of our master and then performing it on our own initiative. This is what a leader does. The altar of sacrifice was ten times larger in Solomon's temple than in Moses' tabernacle. Moses' giving was commanded and precisely calculated. Solomon gave unlimited sacrifices unto the lord. The Bible says these were innumerable.

When Solomon did these elaborate sacrifices, the Lord met him. No one ever had been given a privilege from God as Solomon was. God told Solomon to ask Him anything he desired and God would grant it. That is a very outstanding privilege. But it was granted because of Solomon's unsolicited giving. Giving beyond what is commanded activates a realm of blessings beyond the basic.

Many have moved into the basic truth of tithing. They obeyed this Biblical command. You are now ready to go beyond that level and offer unto God without being told to do so. Take charge of your possessions. Do not let them rule you.

Chapter Fifteen

Beyond Gethsemane

HE SETTING SUN over Jerusalem brought to a close more than just another day. Soon the first morning rays of a new era will pierce through the gloom of legalism, judgement, and condemnation. This morning will never have an evening, nor will the sun ever set on this eternal day. Multitudes of prophecies, types, shadows, and allegories have waited many years for their fulfilment. In a matter of hours the documents of an eternal covenant will be signed in Holy Blood. This is what Gethsemane is hosting.

In the stillness of a serene evening, the groans of one who is God in the flesh are reverberating throughout the beautiful garden. Neither heaven above nor earth below have ever witnessed such sounds of intercession. These prayers will never be heard again. They are finalizing the past and birthing an eternal future. It is the Lamb of God taking on the sins of the whole world, past, present, and future.

While heaven is holding its breath in glorious anticipation, hell is panicking in horror. Its authority and dominion will be stripped away in a matter of a few hours. Hell has an emergency board meeting to plan how they can lie more proficiently to counteract this great victory of Christ the King. Just imagine Lucifer as the chairman of this meeting, being the father of lies. Imagine all the demons running the various departments of the kingdom of darkness and lying about everything they have done on their reports.

The patriarchs and prophets are finally seeing the fulfilment of their ministries and life sacrifices. The Messiah has come to usher in heaven's kingdom on earth through redeemed saints. The final perfect sacrifice is about to be made. The sacrifice not only will pay for past and future debts, but will purchase a people perfected in God's image. The sacrifice is extremely big, because it is Jesus who is God in the flesh. That is big!

The animal kingdom was sighing with relief, but at the same time experiencing a degree of disappointment. Relieved because they will not have to give their lives for sacrifice any longer. Disappointed because they will no longer be the type and shadow of the awesome Lamb of God. This Lamb of God is the final and complete sacrifice once and for all, forever.

The very one who brought this garden out of a messy chaos is now kneeling in its midst. Soon the tree He created will suspend Him between heaven and earth. The man He created, formed intelligently with His hand, gave Him breath, will now take His away. What painter with brush and canvas could even begin to capture such mystery and depth of this divine event?

He who had no sin, now was becoming sin. He who needed no sacrifice, now is one. He who could have damned us in our sins, is damned himself. He is full of mercy but not for Himself. He is filled with grace but does not use it for Himself. He could have used His power to be glorified and exalted. But instead, He used His power to die for us and be resurrected.

All this is too marvellous for words, too profound for song. What music notes could ever be arranged to express even a little of such excellent glory. Heaven itself cannot contain Him. It is spilling over to earth with such depth of love only Gethsemane could witness that night. But even at that, earth shudders at such wonder. It could not carry such love and glory without shaking with respect to the creator.

All hell was summoned by the judge of the ages to appear at Calvary. Lucifer and all the hordes of hell has to appear to witness the signing of the New Covenant. Spirits of depression, oppression, sickness, disease, and infirmities of all sorts had to be there. Demonic forces of injustice, corruption, and iniquity were summoned to the cross.

Darkness covered the earth. The very light was obscured by the arriving hordes of hell. The earthly heavens were blackened with man's sins, which had to be present at the cross where each would experience a nail hole through it.

Soon the very earth created by the Lord would quake. The hard rocks would split and crumble at this act and sight. When innocent and divine blood touches the earth, the earth has no ability to embrace it but react.

At this point Jesus is on His third prayer. Great drops of sweat as drops of blood fall from His sacred brow. How could we ever comprehend the weight of sin that was being down loaded on Him? He not only bore all our sins but *became* sin. In those moments of the cross, Jesus experienced every sin known to mankind. He took all our sins to the cross. Only He qualified, being the sinless son of God, to do this.

What was such excruciating agony Jesus experienced about? Remember, this is Jesus who is truly God in human flesh and form. Could our sins exceed His capacity to bear them without wavering? Were they a bit too much for Jesus? Surely mere humans could not have had the capacity to inflict the Almighty with something to cause Him agony. He had no fear of death. No physical pain could be too much for one who had all authority and power over it. Nothing we could do could possibly make the eternal crumble.

The human-inflicted stripes on His back, the crown of thorns, the spitting on His face, the mockery by humans whom God called a vapour, and welting green grass, could not possibly bring such severe agony to Jesus. Then what did?

Of course Jesus felt the pain and was touched with the feeling of our infirmity. He felt the bruising for our iniquity and the chastisement of our peace was upon Him. He was wounded for our transgressions. He was fully aware of the dramatic sacrifice He would have to make to successfully process our salvation. As the son of God, He became the son of man so that we, as sons of man, could become sons of God. His love for fallen humanity and the fact that He could fix that was the anaesthetic that numbed the pain. Yes, He could do this.

Jesus prayed the same prayer three times. The Father always heard and answered His prayer. There was no sin problem here, no lack of faith. His status and relations with the Father were excellent. But all He got was silence from heaven.

It was heaven's intentional silence that brought about the most painful agony. Jesus came from the bosom of the Father and now it seemed like all that was disconnected, broken off. He knew He was His Father's only beloved and begotten son, but why the silence now when He needed Him the most? How could this be good for Jesus?

This sense of abandonment was expressed on the cross when Jesus cried out, "My God, my God, why hast thou forsaken me?" Jesus could understand those He blessed running off with the blessing and forgetting Him. He could put up with being disappointed with His very own sleepy disciples. He came to His own, but they rejected Him. He handled this really well and even ministered to their monetary needs. But this silence was one of a kind and painful beyond words.

Heaven's silence was intentional. Up until now, Jesus said, "As the servant of God, I only do what I see the Father do; I only say what I hear the Father say." But it's transition time. It's time for graduation from the status of a servant to kingship. Jesus must make this decision alone. All alone.

The Father could not command Jesus to go to the cross. It had to be His decision. If the Father demanded Jesus to go to the cross and (of course) Jesus obeyed, it would have locked Him into a servant status. It was necessary for Jesus to die on the cross as the king, not as a servant. What is sown, also is harvested. In what status Jesus dies is the status in which He resurrects.

What should you do when you've prayed, waited, gone from seminar to seminar, did all you know how to do, and heaven is still silent? No voice, no sign, no vision. No prophetic word. Just silence. You are feeling betrayed, frustrated, and even angry with God. There are multitudes of believers who are genuinely sincere, loving God, serving Him and His Church, but they become discouraged when they experience heaven's silence. When their Gethsemane comes, they become despondent, pull back from God, and even quit serving Him.

Even though Gethsemane's silence makes no sense to the natural mind, it is actually designed for advancement. When heaven is silent, it is because it wants you to step into kingship and do what you know is right. If God tells you what to do, that means you are still in a servant status and not rulership. Kings do not wait to be told what to do; they just do it. In a servanthood status, we wait to be commanded so we can obey. In kingship, we have learned the heart of our master by now and take initiative to do what we know is His will.

A moment comes when groaning comes to an end and action takes over. Gethsemane is a place we pass through but in which we do not settle. While heaven was still silent, Jesus walked out of the garden. In essence, He walked out of one status and into another. No more would He be a servant. He was now headed for kingship and the throne via the cross. He alone had to choose to lay down His life and pick it up again. He was not forcibly murdered. He could have called twelve legions of heavenly hosts to assist Him but He didn't. He was moving into kingship and therefore did not need heaven's command, but only initiative to do what was God's will.

Jesus did not stay for a long time in Gethsemane. He did not hang on the cross for long. In fact, the Roman soldiers were surprised to find Him expired so early. He did not wait for death to take Him. He commended His spirit to His

Father. He had no intention of lying around the tomb among the dead. Jesus sent an angel to put His resurrection apparel in the tomb before He got there. He was not going to wear grave clothes looking for pity. Jesus left the grave clothes neatly folded in the tomb. Fold up your grave clothes and leave them in the tomb. Don't keep wearing them just to show people what hardships you went through. The King's robes are much better. No one gets to sit on the throne with grave clothes.

In 1 Samuel 16:1, God told Samuel to quit mourning for so long, fill the empty horn of oil, and anoint a new king for a new day. This message is for thousands who are stuck in mourning, waiting for a word from God. Rise up like a king; don't wait to be commanded as a servant. Be the king Jesus made you and take the action you know is right. Heaven's silence is a sign for your graduation. God is not ignoring you but giving you the privilege to take action and be catapulted into a new level. Silence may not have a sound but always has a message.

Take initiative and go beyond obedience!

CPSIA information can be obtained
at www.ICGtesting.com
Printed in the USA
LVOW11s1356130617

537958LV00001B/82/P